A PRIVATE GUIDEBOOK TO PRESIDENTIAL MUSEUMS

AN IDEAL FAMILY VACATION

Thomas B. Czerner M.D
Cynthia Wax Czerner

INTRODUCTION

Ten Presidents
George Washington
Abraham Lincoln
Woodrow Wilson
Herbert Hoover
Franklin D. Roosevelt
Harry S. Truman
Dwight D. Eisenhower
John F. Kennedy
Ronald Reagan
William J. Clinton

On our cross-country trip visiting these Presidential Museums and meeting with their directors or staffs we were struck by how deeply these ten presidents transformed the United States of America and how indelibly they altered the lives of its people. It also convinced us of the vital role that Presidential Museums perform in preserving their stories. We began this journey with some skepticism, expecting that we might find extravagant temples built primarily to enhance the prestige of their namesakes. While evidence of narcissism may be found in some of the recent exhibitions, we were impressed with the overall candor of the museums we visited. We were fascinated by stories that we never knew or had forgotten; and we were surprised by previously classified documents and tape recordings that shed new – and sometimes unfavorable – light on the history that continues to shape our future.

Each President's chapter in this guidebook is followed by a collection of travel tips, including suggestions for lodging, restaurants, attractions and other fun things to see and do near each museum. Armed with this information, we believe you will be ready for an ideal family vacation – a great getaway as well as a shared adventure in learning. In the meantime, we hope this armchair tour will lead to a deeper appreciation of the rare privilege and profound responsibilities that stem from being a citizen of this beautiful country.

"I want people to learn from the past so they can better create their own future."

Franklin D. Roosevelt

"If we forget what we did, we won't know who we are."

Ronald Reagan

TABLE OF CONTENTS

INTRODUCTION   iii

GEORGE WASHINGTON   6
Travel Tips   19

ABRAHAM LINCOLN   26
Travel Tips   36

THOMAS WOODROW WILSON   42
Travel Tips   51

HERBERT HOOVER   55
Travel Tips   63

FRANKLIN D. ROOSEVELT   67
Travel Tips   82

HARRY S. TRUMAN   88
Travel Tips   102

DWIGHT D. EISENHOWER   107
Travel Tips   124

JOHN F. KENNEDY   129
Travel Tips   160

RONALD REAGAN   165
Travel Tips   183

WILLIAM J. CLINTON   189
Travel Tips   200

NOTES: 205

GEORGE WASHINGTON

1st President: 1789 – 1797

First Lady: Martha Dandridge Custis Washington

This guided excursion through U.S. history begins at George Washington's Mount Vernon on the Virginia bank of the Potomac River. As you set foot on these grounds, you feel as though you are stepping back through time into 18th century Colonial America. The mansion, plantation and surrounding woodlands appear just as they would have to the young man who inherited this property when the idea of a United States of America had not yet crossed anyone's mind.

EARLY YEARS: George Washington was born not far from Mount Vernon in 1732. Like his father and grandfather, he grew up as a proud citizen of the British Colony of Virginia. His father died when George was only 11, which meant that George could not follow in the steps of his older half-brothers who had attended college in Great Britain. George inherited a small Virginia property called "Ferry Farm" and lived there for a while with his mother; however, he soon left to join his half-brother Lawrence who had inherited a home here at Mount Vernon. Lawrence was ill with tuberculosis and was grateful to have his younger brother's help with this plantation.

This relationship proved to be a blessing for George. When he and Lawrence travelled to the Island of Barbados together, George contracted a mild case of smallpox, giving him immunity to the often-fatal disease. This later protected him when many of his troops became infected with the virus. Lawrence married Ann Fairfax, whose family belonged to the upper crust of British society. The Fairfax tie led to George's first job as a surveyor at age 16 and would also help him latter in life. He earned enough as a surveyor to purchase more land.

The exhibit seen below shows an accurate likeness of George at 19 with his fine English clothes, brass telescope and English pistol; all of which were paid for with tobacco sent from Virginia to Great Britain.

MILITARY AMBITIONS: At age 20, young George petitioned to join the Virginia regiment of the British armed forces. The British were at war with the French, competing for land in the Ohio Valley. Washington was appointed to accompany the British General, Edward Braddock, who was leading two regiments of British troops into the contested area. Along the way, they were ambushed by French soldiers and Indians hiding in the forest. In the panic that followed many men were killed and General Braddock was mortally wounded. George Washington ignored heavy gunfire, stayed astride his white horse, rallied the General's cowering troops, and led them out of the ambush saving many lives. Word of Washington's bravery spread to colonies beyond the borders of Virginia, and he was elevated to the position of Colonel of the Virginia Regiment, a position he held from the age of 23 until he retired from military service three years later, when he was only 26 years old.

MARRAGE: In 1759, George Washington married the wealthy widow, Martha Dandridge Custis and planned to spend the rest of his life at Mount Vernon as a socialite, farmer and businessman. By then Lawrence had died and George was leasing the plantation from Lawrence's widow, Ann. George inherited Mount Vernon at the age of 29, when Ann died in 1761.

George's marriage provided him with money to enlarge the mansion at Mount Vernon as well as to expand his acreage on the property. The marriage also gave him the social prominence necessary to become a member of the Virginia legislature. However, he remained focused on developing Mount Vernon, which he now shared with Martha and two children from her former marriage.

George and Martha gave frequent dinner parties at Mount Vernon as illustrated in the painting above. Washington began spending so much money on his home and plantation that he suddenly found himself in debt. As a result, he began to concentrate on the business of the plantation.

BUSINESS MAN FARMER: The old practice of trading tobacco for British goods had become a losing proposition. British merchants not only set the price that Colonists would receive for their crops, but also the price that Colonists would pay for the goods they ordered from England. This one-sided arrangement always favored the merchants and disadvantaged the planters. Washington began to sell his products locally in order to lessen his dependence on British agents. He studied the soil, learned the latest farming techniques and found that by rotating crops he could farm wheat, corn, soybeans and many other crops that could be sold and consumed in Virginia. Gradually, he began to replace tobacco with lucrative crops that did not deplete the soil. He wrote, *"I hope that someday or another, we shall become a store house and granary for the world."*

Washington did not limit his unbounded energy to farming alone. He initiated a series of successful endeavors at Mount Vernon, including flour milling, horse breeding, spinning and weaving. The museum contains a replica of the Gristmill that he built to grind flour not only from his own grain, but also from grain of other planters who followed his farming example.

Washington also started a commercial fishery, adding fresh Potomac herring to his list of profitable commodities. Later, he started a successful whiskey distillery as well.

These challenging projects commanded his full attention and Mount Vernon fulfilled Washington's life's ambition. He could not have imagined that he would one day be a war-hardened General leading a rebellion against the vaunted British Army or that he would become the first President of an independent nation.

CONFLICT WITH GREAT BRITIAIN: In the late 1760's, the relationship between England and the American Colonies grew tense. The British Parliament raised taxes on the Colonies in order to help pay for the English war against the French. The Colonists refused to pay these taxes unless they had representatives in the British Parliament who would look out for their interests.   "No taxation without representation" became a rallying cry. A museum exhibit displays a popular tavern song of the time: *And tell King George we'll pay no Taxes on his foreign tea."*

Washington took part in protests complaining that taxation without representation violated his rights as a British citizen. He began to lead boycotts and organize peaceful protests, hoping that the British would change their policies. He warned, "Continued suppression of American liberties would lead to armed rebellion." In 1773, a band of angry Colonists dressed as Indians boarded an English ship docked in Boston Harbor and threw its load of tea overboard. Although Washington did not participate in the "Boston Tea Party", he realized that rebellion had reached a breaking point when the British responded with a new set of laws that further restricted Colonists' freedoms.

REVOLUTION: The Colonies were now determined to break free from their British bondage and declare their independence. In June, of

1775, Washington accepted the post of Commander in Chief of the Continental Army.

At age 43, he left the comfort of Mount Vernon and went to war once more. This time, however, he would not fight with the British, but against them.

Statue of King George, New York 1776

On July 6, 1776, Washington was with his army in New York when he received a copy of the Declaration of Independence. He read the document aloud to a huge crowd in front of City Hall, who proceeded to tear down a statute of King George III. The bronze was melted down and shaped into more than 42,000 musket balls for Washington's army to use against the British.

The soldiers did this not only to demonstrate their hatred for the British King. They did it from necessity. They had little or no money to buy the ammunition, supplies and equipment necessary to fight a war. The Continental Congress that had declared their independence had not formed a central government able to levy taxes and support a national army. General Washington literally had to beg for money to feed, clothe and supply his troops. They were brave men, but they were going up against well-equipped and experienced British soldiers.

An interactive map at the museum allows visitors to follow the progress of Washington's war, which was largely a war of attrition. Without sufficient men, arms or supplies to score decisive victories, he inflicted as much damage on the enemy as possible and then retreated to fight another day. Washington's tattered army walked from battle to battle, often with bleeding feet wrapped in rags when their shoes wore out.

By December of 1776 there was little to show for their efforts and the outlook seemed bleak. In that bitter winter, Washington rallied his despairing troops and led them across the Delaware River to attack the enemy at Trenton, New Jersey.

He was certainly not standing upright in a small boat as the famous painting above suggests. In fact, this was a surprise attack. The troops crossed the Delaware River crouching low on large, flat-bottomed boats and won their first major victory of the war. The success at Trenton raised the morale of his troops as well as the hopes of the country. The victory also caused the French to believe that George Washington's army might defeat the British, and they began sending weapons and troops to help Washington win the war.

VICTORY: In 1778, the French formally recognized the independence of the United States, and in 1781 French soldiers and seamen helped to force a surrender of British General Cornwallis and more than 7,000 British troops at Yorktown, Virginia.

Although the victory at Yorktown brought the fighting to an end, the British still held New York and other U.S. territory until a peace treaty was signed in Paris, France in 1783. The Paris Treaty ended the American Revolutionary War and gave formal recognition to the United States as an independent country.

Benjamin Franklin (2nd from left) at the signing of
The Paris Peace Treaty
(Painting by Carl Wilhelm Anton Seiler)

NEW CONSTITUTION: Washington returned to Mount Vernon at the age of 51. Although he was technically retired, he lobbied hard for a new Constitution. He wanted the new nation to have a strong central government with taxing power. The delegates at the Constitutional Convention chose Washington to preside over their contentious debates.

OUR FIRST PRESIDENT: When it was time to choose the first President of the United States, the voting for George Washington was unanimous. He took the oath of office on April 30, 1789.

During Washington's first term, two cabinet members had rival views of American's future.

Alexander Hamilton
Secretary of Treasury

Thomas Jefferson
Secretary of State

Alexander Hamilton, Secretary of the Treasury, believed in a strong national government with states focusing mainly on local issues. Hamilton saw American society becoming less centered on agriculture and developing into a more urban and industrial society.

Thomas Jefferson, Secretary of State, wanted the exact opposite: He feared a strong central government and preferred one in which State rights would be dominant over Federal laws. Jefferson believed that America would remain primarily a rural and agricultural nation. These different views split politicians into two camps that fought bitterly, often ridiculing and lying about their opponents.

In Washington's second term, it seemed likely that the United States would go to war again with Great Britain. England was not abiding by the Treaty of Paris. Its troops had not left America as the treaty required and its Navy continued to seize American ships, sailors and merchandize trading with France, England's enemy. England also continued to levy unfair tariffs on goods coming from America.

Washington sent Chief Justice John Jay to negotiate with the British to solve these issues. The "Jay Treaty" that Justice Jay negotiated was unpopular with much of the Congress and most of the American public, who felt more warmly toward France than to England. Although Great Britain agreed to compensate American merchants for goods the British had confiscated, nearly every other clause of the agreement favored England. Indeed, most of Great Britain's unfair trade practices continued as before.

Washington signed the flawed treaty because he knew that the U.S. was not ready to fight and wanted to avoid another war. The Senate ratified the treaty by a small margin. When the House threatened not to fund the treaty's implementation, Washington argued the Constitution requires the House to fund any treaty that has been ratified by the Senate. He ultimately won this bitter political battle that had pitted the "Federalist Party" that favored Alexander Hamilton's support for the treaty against the "Jeffersonian Republican Party" that joined its leader, Thomas Jefferson, in vehemently opposing it.

In his farewell address, Washington warned of the danger posed by political parties. He was afraid that politicians would be more concerned with advancing the interests of their party then with meeting the needs of their country. He also warned against foreign alliances and entanglements, which he felt would draw the U.S. into wars having no benefit for our country. He even refused to support the French in 1793 in their war with the British, even though French troops helped Washington's army to win independence for America.

As our first President, George Washington established precedents with everything that he did. Fortunately, he showed meticulous respect for the limits of executive power. By declining a third term in office, he demonstrated his resolve that there should always be a peaceful transition from one elected leader to the next.

SLAVERY: While the colonists fought for their liberty, they continued to buy and sell slaves, who were considered "property" rather than human beings. Even Washington owned slaves and kept them in sparse living quarters near his opulent home. Visitors to Mount Vernon can see their meager sleeping and cooking facilities and their small allotment of food and clothing.

Slave Quarters

Sleeping Quarters

Slave Kitchen

A year's clothing and
a day's food

Although Washington did not speak out against slavery, his will provided that all of his slaves would be set free upon his death. Washington died on December 14, 1799 and, although his slaves became "free," they remained second-class members of a society unaccustomed to seeing people of their color walking among them.

At the next Museum on this tour, we will see how the unconscionable institution of slavery very nearly tore our nation apart. We will now travel from Mount Vernon on the East Coast to Abraham Lincoln's Museum in Springfield, Illinois.

Visiting George Washington's Mount Vernon

**3200 Mount Vernon Memorial Highway,
Mount Vernon, VA 22121**

Telephone: (800) 429-1520 or 703-780-2000

Website: www.mountvernon.org

Museum Hours:
> November through February: 9am-4pm
> March, September and October: 9am-5pm
> April through August: 8am-5pm
> Open on all holidays; only closed for inclement weather

Admission Fees when purchased at the Museum:
> $18 Adult (12-61) :
> $17 Senior (62+with ID)
> $9 Child (6-11), younger than 6 are free
> Best to come in the morning if you want to visit the Mansion

Online Admission Fees:
> $1 less than above in each category to encourage online buying; Since tickets are NOT REFUNDABLE and are DATE SPECIFIC, we recommend that you buy tickets at the museum, and not online; If you do buy online, REMEMBER TO BRING YOUR TICKET; Also, you will need to pick a time to visit the Mansion. Best to allow at least an hour after you plan to arrive

Annual Passes:
> $28 Adult (12 and older) $12 Child (6-11); If you plan to come more than once a year, this is a good deal. The annual pass gives you admittance to Mount Vernon for one year from the day of your first visit. If you get an individual ticket and decide you

want to come again in the same year, even at the end of the day, you can walk up to the ticket line with your ticket stub and pay the difference between the price you paid for your ticket and the price of the annual pass. (No senior discount for annual passes)

Special Event Tickets:

To see what special events are available on the day of your visit, go to the website: **www.mountvernon.org** and click on "Calendar" at the top of the page. We suggest not buying these tickets online since these are also NOT REFUNDABLE, and if you are late, you probably would not be admitted to the event even though you already paid.

Special Rates for Adult Groups of 20 or more and Student Groups:

Reservations are required for Adult and Student groups. Call (703) 799-8688 or email: groups@mountvernon.org

Parking:

Parking is free for Mount Vernon visitors

Accessibility:

Standard, non-motorized wheelchairs and walkers are available free of charge inside the Ford Orientation Center on a first-come basis. It is suggested that you call (703) 780-2000 if you have any special needs. Certified service animals or service animals-in-training are welcome.

Eating at Mount Vernon:

There are two places to eat:

1. The Mount Vernon Inn Restaurant

Reservations are suggested for dinner. Call 703-780-0011 to make your reservation or book it on Opentable.com.

Lunch: Mon – Sat: 11am–3:30 pm
Dinner: Mon-Thurs: 5pm-8:30pm; Fri – Sat: 5pm–9pm
Sunday Brunch: 11pm–7pm
Happy Hour: Mon-Fri: 4pm-8pmv

2. Food Court

The Food Court offers a quick alternative for breakfast, lunch, and snacks. Hot items served until one hour before closing: Nov-Feb: 10am– 4:30pm; Mar, Sep & Oct: 9:30am–5:30pm; Apr-

Aug: 8:30am–6pm

What to Wear & Bring: Mount Vernon recommends walking shoes and comfortable clothing. Be aware that Virginia can be hot and humid in the summer so please bring bottled water; other beverages and food must stay outside Mount Vernon's gates. Large bags, backpacks, etc. are strongly discouraged.

Photography: Photography is permitted in all areas except for the Mansion, Museum, and the gallery in the Education Center featuring the General's dentures (contrary to common myth, George Washington's dentures were not made of wood; they were made of bone and were tied to his teeth with wires).

Dogs Allowed: Dogs are allowed at Mount Vernon if kept on a leash and never left alone; however non-service dogs cannot be taken into buildings such as the Mansion or the museum.

Suggestions for Lodging:

Note from Authors, Cynthia & Tom:

In our first edition, we listed several hotels in Alexandria and other areas close to Mount Vernon even though we were not thrilled with their caliber. In this edition, we decided to include great hotels in Washington D.C. because they are not that far away from Mount Vernon, especially if you have a car. Washington DC is about a 30-minute drive to and from Mt. Vernon. Public transit takes much longer (at least an hour) but we believe that the extra travel time is worth it if you have a nice place to lodge. We list one hotel in Alexandria in case you have young kids and/or pets and want to be closer to Mount Vernon.

We also included additional Bed and Breakfast Inns both in D.C. and Alexandria. Please check the policies of B&Bs before booking with them because they often differ from those of hotels, and please read our NOTES at the end of this book on the pros and cons of staying in B&Bs versus hotels.

Embassy Circle Guest House:
 2224 R Street. NW, Washington D.C. 20008
 (202) 232-7744 or toll free (877) 232-7744
 Website: **www.dcinns.com**
 10 stunning rooms with en suite bathrooms; 2 night minimum;
 Free breakfast; Happy hour with wine and beer; Adults only
 Near Woodrow Wilson's D.C. house: 2340 S. St. NW, Wash.
 Wilson's house: (202) 387-4062; Tue-Sun: 10am-4pm: $10 Adults

Woodley Park Guest House:
 2647 Woodley Road, NW, Washington, D.C. 20008:
 (202) 232-7744 or toll free (877) 232-7744
 Website: **www.dcinns.com**
 Owned by same people who own Embassy Circle Guest House;
 Equally stunning property however all rooms do not have ensuite
 bathrooms.

The Jefferson:
 1200 16th Street, NW, Washington, D.C. 20036
 (202) 448-2300; Website: **www.Jeffersondc.com**
 Downtown, four blocks from the White House
 Free Wi-Fi; Free bottled water; paid parking (currently $45);
 Hotel Bar: the Quill; Hotel Restaurant: the Plume
 Dogs allowed (no fee currently charged for pets)

Capella Washington D.C., Georgetown:
 1050 31st Street, NW, Washington, D.C. 20007
 (202) 617-2400; Website: **www.capellahotels.com**
 Free Wi-Fi; paid parking (currently $48);
 Rooftop pool but not heated
 Hotel Restaurant, the Grill Room

216 Bed & Breakfast:
 216 South Fayette Street, Alexandria, VA 22314:
 (703) 548-8118; Website: **www.216bandb.com**
 This is a beautiful home in Old Town Alexandria
 The owners live next door, so the entire B&B is rented out
 It has three bedrooms, 2 bathrooms, a private patio
 Free parking for one car; free breakfast; free Wife; no smoking

Lorien Hotel & Spa, a Kimpton Hotel
>   1600 King Street, Alexandria, VA 22314
>   (703) 894-3434; Website: **www.lorienhotelandspa.com**
>   Free Wi-Fi if you sign up for their loyalty program
>   Pets welcome (no fee); also have floors with no pets
>   Paid parking (currently $30); paid breakfast;

Suggestions for Restaurants

King Street Cafe (breakfast & lunch place)
>   1018 King Street, Alexandria, VA 222314
>   (703) 549-3717
>   Mon-Sat: 8am-5pm; Closed Sundays; metered street parking

Ray's the Steaks
>   2300 Wilson Blvd, Arlington, VA 22201
>   (703) 841-7297 (Street level in the Navy League Building)
>   Website: **www.raysthesteaks.com**; **Dinner only**
>   Daily from 5pm-10pm; reservations encouraged

Rasika: (Indian)
>   1190 New Hampshire Ave. NW, Washington, D.C. 20037
>   (202) 466-2500; Website: **www.rasikarestaurant.com/westen**
>   Lunch: Mon-Fri: 11:30am-2:30pm;
>   Dinner: Mon-Thu: 5:30pm-10:30; Fri-Sat: 5pm-11pm

Bistro Cacao: (French)
>   320 Massachusetts Ave, NE, Washington, DC 20002
>   (202) 546-4737: Website: **www.bistrocacao.com**
>   Open Daily
>   **Lunch**: Mon-Fri: 11:30am-3pm; **Brunch**: Sat-Sun: 10pm-3pm
>   **Dinner:** Sun-Thu: 5pm-10pm; Fri-Sat: 5pm-11pm

Marcel's by Robert Wiedmaier (Fine dining: Belgian-French)
>   2401 Pennsylvania Ave NW, Washington DC 20037
>   (202) 296-1166; Website: **www.marcelsdc.com**
>   Jackets required
>   Open 7 days a week for dinner only
>   Mon-Thu: 5pm-10pm; Fri-Sat: 5am-11pm; Sun: 5pm-9:30pm

Attractions in the Area

Historic King Street in Old Town Alexandria:

So many great restaurants and stores

A free trolley runs up down the street every 15-20 minutes until 10pm; Visitors can take that trolley to the metro station to go to Washington, D.C. or to Mount Vernon

Smithsonian Museums (SMs): Information for all SMs & ZOO:

Admission is Free, but parking is not free

General number for all SMs: (202) 633-1000

See more SMs & a map at the Website: **www.si.edu** than listed

All SMs close on Dec 25: Unless noted, **10am-5:30 daily**

National Air and Space Museum

6th and Independence Ave., SW (National Mall)

Museum of National History

10th Street and Constitution Ave (National Mall)

American Art Museum (11:30am-7pm)

8th and F Streets, NW (downtown/Chinatown)

National Museum of American History

1300 Constitution Ave. NW between 12th and 14th Streets

National Zoo

3001 Connecticut Ave NW, Washington, DC 20008

Parking is $22; Website: **www.nationalzoo.si.edu**

National Gallery of Art (free admission)

Constitution Ave and 6th Ave, Washington D.C. 20002

West Building and East Building; on the National Mall

(202) 737-4215; Website: **www.nga.gov**

Art donated to the American people by Andrew W. Mellon

Mon-Sat: 10am-5pm: Sun: 11am-6pm: Closed Dec 25 & Jan 1

For special needs, call (202) 842-6690

Tours of Capitol Hill and the White House

Call your local Congressional Representatives

They can get you tickets, but they need advance notice;

Monuments for Presidents Washington, Lincoln & Roosevelt
Website: **www.nps.gov**; see the map of the Mall

Washington Monument
2 15th Street NW, Washington D.C.
Need tickets to go inside but they are free (there is a $1.50 service
charge per ticket only for online ticketing)
To get tickets in person, go to the Washington Monument Lodge,
which is on 15th street at the base of the Washington Monument
The Washington Monument is open every day except July 4th
and Dec. 25: Winter Hours: 9am-5pm;
Summer Hours (Memorial Day to Labor Day): 9am-10pm

Lincoln Memorial and Reflecting Pool
2 Lincoln Memorial Circle NW, Washington D.C

Franklin and Eleanor Roosevelts' Memorial
400 West Bason Drive SW, Washington D.C

Potomac Riverboat Company
1 Cameron Street, Alexandria, VA 22314
(703) 684-0580 or toll free (877) 511-2628
Website: www.potomacriverboatco.com
Sightseeing tours/taxis to several Washington DC monuments
A Mount Vernon package is available that includes a round trip
water taxi ride and a ticket to Mount Vernon (They pick you up
after 4 hours for the return trip.)
The cost and timing depends on the tour or taxi you choose plus
other factors, so it is best to review these on their website

ABRAHAM LINCOLN

16th President   1861 – 1865

First Lady   Mary Todd Lincoln

Abe Lincoln's story is an American legend, confirming that anyone in this country can rise to the top. Born in an obscure log cabin in Kentucky's western frontier, Lincoln became a popular, self-educated country lawyer, a state legislator, a United States Congressman and the President who saved America from self-destruction.

To be sure, Lincoln would not have reached such prominence had he not been white and male. Women's suffrage would not be achieved until early in the next century and the battles for broader civil rights would go on even longer. The burning issue of Lincoln's day, however, was the unconscionable plight of African slaves.

When you walk into the Lincoln Museum, you are greeted by the lifelike figures of President Lincoln and his family standing in front of the 1861 White House. The figures are accurate to the smallest detail. Also present, leaning against a pillar is John Wilkes Booth, the man who four years later would be Lincoln's assassin.

As you move through the exhibits, you will realize what a divided and angry country Lincoln was called upon to lead. You will see scathing cartoons of him and listen to the sharp words that were written and spoken about him. Above all, however, you will see dramatic portrayals of a wise leader using his innate talent with words. Among the more moving examples in the Museum is his first inaugural address, ending with his ringing appeal to the "better angels of our nature."

FROM BOYHOOD TO STATESMAN: These full-scale dioramas of Lincoln's childhood home are not rough approximations. The boy's face and figure are as close to Lincoln's actual appearance at that age as the latest technology permits. We were told that the cabin is of the same age, material and design as the original.

The portrayals of young Abe reading by firelight, and pondering a book in his hand, reflect the key to Lincoln's success. Abe Lincoln loved stories. From his childhood on, he loved to read them, listen to them and to tell them to anyone willing to listen. His fame was the result of his hard work and winning personality, but it was especially due to his wonderful way with words. His love of stories and his knack for storytelling turned many strangers and even his adversaries into friends.

Lincoln gained local recognition in the 1830s as an Illinois State legislator and again, from 1846 to 1848, when he served one term as an Illinois Representative in the U.S. Congress. While in Congress, he spoke out against slavery. Although that inhumane bondage was a blight on the conscience of the nation, it was also the life-blood of the Southern plantation economy.

The Museum's life-size diorama of a typical slave auction conveys much more than one might glean from reading the grim statistics of slavery. It portrays the heartbreak of a family torn apart and sold to separate slave owners.

After his term in Congress was over, Lincoln returned to practice law in a brick, two-story building in Springfield, Illinois. His well-preserved office is a popular attraction within walking distance of the

Lincoln Museum.

THE LINCOLN/DOUGLAS DEBATES: Lincoln first gained national prominence in 1858, when the newly formed, anti-slavery Republican Party nominated him to run for the U.S. Senate against the Democrat, Stephen Douglas. The seven debates between Lincoln and Douglas became the most famous political debates in American history.

Although Lincoln lost that race, his vehement opposition to the expansion of slavery into the new territories of Kansas and Nebraska energized the fledgling Republican Party just in time for the 1860 Presidential election.

SLAVERY AS A CAMPAIGN ISSUE: In February 1860, Lincoln was invited to speak to a group of prominent Republicans at a new school in New York City, The Cooper Union College. In his famous "Cooper Union speech," Lincoln faced the issue of slavery head on. He rejected *"groping for some middle ground between the right and the wrong."*

Neither of the declared candidates for the Republican nomination for President, (William Seward and Salmon Chase), had taken such an uncompromising stand against slavery. Perhaps more than any other factor, Lincoln's powerful Cooper Union speech propelled him ahead of those more experienced politicians to become the Republican Presidential nominee for the 1860 election. (Once elected, he appointed these former Republican rivals to become members of his Cabinet.) However, Lincoln's bold stand against slavery had solidified the opposition of the Southern States and threatened to cost him the election.

One of the most interesting exhibits at the Lincoln Museum is an amusing television analysis of the complicated 1860 election narrated by the late Tim Russert. It is presented in the same manner and with the same "high-tech," electoral maps, graphs and running commentary used in modern television reporting of elections.

Lincoln was one candidate in a confusing field of four. The Southern faction of the Democratic Party nominated John Breckenridge who won nearly every vote cast in the South. The Northern Democrats nominated Stephen Douglas, who had previously won the Lincoln/Douglas race for the Senate. Only Missouri voted for Douglas. The new Constitutional Union Party put up John Bell, who won in all of the Border States (Virginia, Kentucky and Tennessee).

In the insightful manner for which he was famous, Tim Russert artfully explains the complex political landscape and the intractable divisions in the country. He sums up the situation with the appropriate remark, "What a mess!"

LINCOLN WINS THE PRESIDENCY: Lincoln carried only Oregon, California and the Northern States. But that gave him more than enough electoral votes to claim victory. He even won the popular vote as well.

He was inaugurated on March 4, 1861 under heavy guard because there had already been many threats against Lincoln's life. Ironically, the Chief Justice of the Supreme Court who administered the oath of office to Lincoln was the same man who wrote the infamous Dred Scott decision, which held that someone of African decent could not be a citizen of the United States.

SOUTHERN STATES REVOLT: Even before Lincoln took the oath of office, seven Southern States (South Carolina, Mississippi,

Florida, Alabama, Georgia, Louisiana and Texas) announced that they had seceded from the Union because they feared that, with Lincoln as President and slavery eliminated, their plantation economy would be ruined. They declared themselves to be a sovereign nation, "The Confederate States of America," and named Jefferson Davis as their provisional President. Four border-states (Virginia, Arkansas, North Carolina and Tennessee) joined in the secession after Lincoln's inauguration. (The Western part of Virginia refused to secede and became a separate state of the Union called West Virginia. It has remained a separate state to this day.)

PRESIDING OVER WAR: President-elect Lincoln and incumbent President Buchanan declared the secession illegal and the stage was set for a war that everyone, both in the North and in the South, expected to win easily. Breathtaking exhibits at the Lincoln Museum make clear how tragically wrong they both were. A four-minute film (one minute for each year of the war) chronicles the ebb and flow of the epic struggle. A pointer at the bottom moves from month to month as the map changes to show the current battle lines and battle locations. As the film and the war progress, a counter clicks off the rapidly rising number of casualties, sometimes thousands in a single day. Before the Civil War was over, more than 600,000 were killed and many more wounded.

The War lasted from April 1861 (the Confederate attack on South Carolina's Fort Sumter) to April 1865 (General Lee's surrender to General Grant at Appomattox, Virginia). It is hard to imagine that our country went to war over the question of whether some of its people should be considered "property" rather than human beings.

THE EMANCIPATION PROCLAMATION: In 1862, while the war raged on, Lincoln told his Cabinet that he proposed to issue an Executive Order called the "Emancipation Proclamation." This was not going to outlaw slavery everywhere. Its purpose was to free slaves residing in the southern states that were not yet under Northern control. Although such an Executive Order did not need the consent of Congress, Lincoln found that he had to overcome the strong resistance of his skeptical Cabinet.

Arguing for Emancipation

The diorama above is a full-scale replica of Lincoln's Cabinet meeting room. Each face and figure in the room is an accurate likeness, as are the wallpaper, furniture and artifacts assembled there. The plaques along the rail inform the visitor of the identity of each cabinet member and the positions they argued as they considered the ramifications of Lincoln's proposed Emancipation Proclamation. The war had been going badly for the North, and Secretary of State Seward felt this proclamation would be seen as a desperate measure to supplement Union troops with southern slaves suddenly freed and allowed to join the Union Army or Navy. Some members of the cabinet thought it would result in further bloodshed, with revenge-seeking slaves turning against their former owners. Others argued it would invite foreign powers to offer their help to the South.

Lincoln prevailed but his Cabinet wanted him to wait until the Union Army had won a significant battle before issuing the proclamation. Previously, the Union Army had been losing nearly all of its battles against the Confederacy. Finally, at the September Battle of Antietam, the Union Army achieved what they were willing to call a "win." The truth is that the battle was not a victory because the incompetent General McClellan only engaged a fraction of his troops and therefore failed to crush the Confederate Army. After a day of fierce fighting in which slightly more troops were killed on the

Confederate side than the Union side, the Confederate Army was the first to withdraw from the battlefield, which gave Lincoln the right to call the battle a win from a military standpoint.

The Emancipation Proclamation took effect on January 1, 1863. Although it freed slaves, as a practical matter, Southern slaves were set free only when the Union army arrived to liberate them. However, none of the dire consequences predicted by its opponents took place. Over 200,000 freed slaves joined the Union Army. Foreign support turned toward the North rather than the South, ending the Confederacy's hopes of international recognition. And yet Lincoln continued to face the scorn of many people in both the South and the North, who thought that freeing slaves was an outrageous betrayal of the slaveholders' right of ownership.

GETTYSBURG: The tide finally began to turn in favor of the Union after it won a series of battles. The battle of Gettysburg was a decisive turning point; three bloody days in which tens of thousands died. Lincoln was not the main speaker at the ceremony that commemorated the casualties of that battle, but his short statement lives on as a powerful reminder of the principles for which our country was founded, *"a new nation, conceived in Liberty, and dedicated to the proposition that all men are created equal."* He resolved *"that government of the people, by the people, and for the people, shall not perish from the earth."*

PRESIDENTIAL ELECTION: Lincoln insisted on having the 1864 election in the midst of the Civil War declaring, *"You can not have free government without elections … if the rebellion could force us to forgo a national election, it might fairly claim to have already conquered and ruined us."*[1] Putting principle ahead of personal pride, he would abide by the election result even though he thought he would probably lose to General McClellan, whom he had relieved of his command and who now was running against him. However, Lincoln won in a landslide.

THE 13TH AMENDMENT: In order to abolish slavery in every state of the Union, Congress passed the 13th amendment to the Constitution on January 31, 1865. Of course, the States still had to ratify

---

[1] The National Park Service website **www.nps.gov/liho:** (Lincoln Home National Historic Site, Illinois)

this amendment before it could become the law of the land.

VICTORY AT LAST: The Union Army defeated the Confederacy in April of 1865.   General Robert E. Lee surrendered in the Battle of Appomattox in Virginia, and the Civil War officially ended.

In his last public speech, as people were celebrating the end of the war, Lincoln addressed a jubilant crowd from a second floor window of the White House, declaring his intention to propose that freed slaves be given the right to vote.

The Last Speech, April 11, 1865

One of those listening to that speech was John Wilkes Booth. For him and for many others, the granting of voting rights was viewed as a step too far.

ASSASINATION: Six days after Lee's surrender, Booth snuck into the Ford Theater in Washington DC where the president sat watching a play with his wife at his side.

Booth assassinated Lincoln during one of the rare moments of relaxation Lincoln was able to experience during his presidency. Lincoln was dead, the war was over and slavery would officially end in December 1865, when the States ratified the 13th Amendment. However, regional bitterness and racial injustice remained.

Unfortunately, Lincoln's successor, Andrew Johnson, did not pursue Lincoln's plans for reconstructing the South and for giving full citizenship to all freed slaves. Instead, Blacks remained second-class citizens, separate and unequal. Lincoln ended slavery, but his assassination put off for far too long the day when all citizens would enjoy the full fruits of liberty. African Americans were not guaranteed equal protection under the law until a century later, when civil rights legislation and voting rights were passed.

In the interval between the lives of George Washington and Abraham Lincoln, the United States had changed remarkably. The country now stretched from Coast to Coast. People were traveling on steamboats and railroads; they were communicating with telegrams; and many of them began to leave their farms to find new opportunities in rapidly growing cities.

At the next Presidential Museum on this tour, we will see that it was not only freed slaves who struggled to gain the protections promised by our Constitution. Women and the working poor demanded their rights as well. Progressive voices began to be heard in 1912, when a rapidly changing America chose Woodrow Wilson to be its new President.

Visiting Abraham Lincoln's Presidential Museum

212 North Sixth Street, Springfield, IL 62701
Main entrance is at Sixth and Jefferson Streets

(800) 610-2094 or (217) 782-5764
Website: www.presidentlincoln.illinois.gov

Museum Hours:
> Mon-Sun: 9am-5pm (Last ticket sold at 4pm
> Closed Thanksgiving Day, Christmas Day and New Year's Day

Museum Admission Fees:
> $15 Adult (16-61)
> $12 Seniors (62+) and Students with ID)
> $10 Military (ID required
> $6 Children (5-15}; Children age 4 and younger are free
> Tickets are **not refundable or exchangeable** - and tickets are **date specific** so we recommend you buy the tickets at the Museum.
> If you decide to buy the tickets in advance, either call the box office: (217) 558-8934 or go to the Museum's website shown above. Currently, the Museum only takes Visa or MasterCard.

Adult Groups: Adult groups of 15 or more must apply in advance to the Springfield Convention and Visitors' Bureau. Ask about a Group Rate. Go **to www.visit-springfieldillinois.com**; click on "group tours" and then click on "make reservations online." Bookings must be confirmed by the Visitors' Bureau to be valid; Allow 4-6 weeks to receive a confirmation; Payment must be received at least 15 days prior to your visit; remember, all sales are final for the specific date reserved; no refunds or exchanges.

Rules for Groups: If the group is late, the tour could be forfeited. Groups should arrive 15 minutes before the scheduled time; the tour bus will be met by Museum personnel, so the Museum asks that people do not get off the bus until then; see the Museum's website under "Group Tours."

School Groups

School groups must also reserve in advance
If 14 or less, email **carol.manning@illinois.gov** 2 wks. before visit.
If 15 or more, follow Adult Group directions above except use the *Visitors Bureau Student/Youth Group Reservation Request Form*
For questions call Alison Warren: (800) 545-7300, Ext. 126 or send an email to: **Alison.warren@springfield.il.us**

Parking: Paid Parking for visitors to the Museum is on Sixth Street between Madison and Mason Streets

Eating at the Museum: A fast food restaurant chain in the building serves sandwiches and salads. Open 10am-4pm daily;

Special Needs: People in wheel chairs can be dropped off at the Museum's main entrance at Sixth & Jefferson; wheel chairs are available in the Museum on a first come basis; motorized wheel chairs are permitted in the Museum.

Rules of the Museum

No backpacks or large bags are permitted
Umbrellas and bags exceeding a size limit of 11x16x8 must be checked as well as headsets, personal stereos & other electronic equipment.
Photos are only permitted in the Plaza area and Mrs. Lincoln's Attic

Suggestions for Lodging

The first three hotels listed are only a short walk from the Lincoln Presidential Museum (~10 minutes)

The State House Inn (an Ascent Collection Hotel)

101 E. Adams Street, Springfield, IL 62701
(217) 528-5100; Website: **www.thestatehouseinn.com**
Free parking, free breakfast (the food isn't great)
No pets; free wi-fi

President Abraham Lincoln, a Doubletree by Hilton

>701 East Adams Street, Springfield, IL 62701
>(217) 544-8800; **www.presidentabrahamlincolnhotel.com**
>Indoor swimming pool, free wi-fi; paid parking, no pets

The Hilton Springfield

>700 East Adams Street, Springfield, IL 62701
>(217) 789-1530; Website: **www.ithappensatthehilton.com**
>Indoor swimming pool, free Wi-fi; pets allowed ($50 fee)
>Nick & Nino's Penthouse Steakhouse at the Hilton (See below)

Drury Inn and Suites (5.9 miles from the Lincoln Presidential Museum)

>3180 S. Dirksen Parkway, Springfield, IL 62703
>(217) 529-3900; Website: **www.druryhotels.com**
>Great place to bring kids and dogs; pet fee is $10 per night
>Free hot breakfast, free Wi-fi; indoor swimming pool

Suggestions for Restaurants

BREAKFAST/LUNCH ONLY

Café MOXO

>411 East Adams Street, Springfield, IL 62701
>(217) 788-8084; Website: **wwwcafemoxo.com**
>Breakfast/Lunch/Pastries/Soups/Salads;/sandwiches
>Mon – Sat: 6:30am – 3pm; gets crowed and can be noisy
>Cafeteria style ordering (go to counter and order)

Incredibly Delicious

>925 South 7th Street, Springfield, IL 62703
>(217) 528-8548; Website: **www.incrediblydelicious.com**
>Bakery Opens: Mon-Sat at 7:30am
>Bakery Closes: Mon at 4pm: Tue-Fri at 5pm & Sat at 3pm
>Lunch: Mon Fri: 11:00am – 2:30pm; Sat: 11am-2pm

LUNCH & DINNER

Flavor of India

>3124 Montvale Drive, Springfield, IL 62704

(217) 787-8122; Open 7 days a week, Lunch & Dinner
Mon – Fri: Lunch 11:00am – 2:30pm; Dinner: 4:30pm – 10pm
Sat-Sun: 11am-10pm (no closure between lunch and dinner);

Darcy's Pint

661 West Stanford Ave., Springfield, IL 62704
(217) 492-8800; Website: **www.darcyspintonline**
Lunch/Dinner: Mon – Thurs: 11:00am – 10pm
Lunch/Dinner: Fri-Sat: 11am – 11pm
Bar Hours: Mon-Sat: 11am-1am
American & Irish Cuisine; Free parking lot but often crowded

DINNER ONLY

Old Luxemburg Inn

1900 South 15th Street, Springfield, IL 62703
(217) 528-0503;
Dinner: Tue–Sun: 4pm – 9pm; Fri–Sat: 4pm–10pm
Great steaks and seafood; American Cuisine; reasonable prices
Not the greatest neighborhood; however they have three free
parking lots with lights and security.

Nick & Nino's Penthouse Steakhouse (at the Hilton Hotel)

700 E. Adams Street, 30th Floors, Springfield, IL 62701
(217) 789-1530; Website: **www.nickandninosspringfield.co**
Tue–Sat: 5:30pm–10pm; Ask for a table near a window
Valet parking for only $3 at the Hilton; enter on Adams Street

COFFEE HOUSE

William Van's Coffee

503 South 7th Street, Springfield, IL 62701
(217) 679-4726
Open 7 days a week from 7am-7pm except Tue: 6am-7pm

Attractions in Springfield

Abraham Lincoln's Home, National Historic Site:

    426 S. 7th Street, Springfield, Il, 62701

    (217) 391-3221; Website: **www.nps.gov/liho**

    Free admission;

    Open Daily 8:30-5: Closed Thanksgiving, Christmas, New Years

Note: You can only enter with a guided tour; tickets are for a particular time and are limited to 15 people per tour on a first-come-basis. The first tour is at 9am and the last is at 4:30pm. On a busy day they may run out of tickets, therefore, we suggest you go to the Visitor Center early. **School groups or all other groups of 15 or more must reserve well in advance with the Springfield Convention and Visitors Bureau, www.visit-springfieldillinois.com**.

Dana-Thomas House: **(Even better than Lincoln's Home)**

    301 E. Lawrence Ave., Springfield, IL 62703

    (217) 782-6776; donation of $10 requested

    Website: **www.dana-thomas.org**

    1902 Prairie-style Frank Lloyd Wright House

    Stained glass, wine cellar, interesting lights, bowling alley

    Only open 4 days; Thu-Sun: 9am-4pm; free parking

    There are guided tours and you can walk into every room

Illinois State Museum:

    502 S. Spring Street, Springfield, 62706

    (217) 782-7386; Free Admission;

    Website: **www.museum.state.il.us**

    Exhibits on history, science plus fun things for kids to do;

    Main Museum: Mon-Sat: 8:30am-5pm; Sun: Noon-5pm

    Play Museum for kids: Mon-Sat: 9:30am-4pm; Sun: 1pm-5pm;

Old State Capitol:

    Old State Capitol Plaza, near 6th & Adams Street.

    217/785-7960; **website: www.state.il.us/hpa/hs/old_capitol.htm**

    State Capitol reconstructed as it was when Lincoln was alive.

    Free tours and admission, however:

    donations of $4 for adults or $10 for a family are suggested

    Hours are seasonal. Please call or check the Website:

    Closed New Year's Day, Martin Luther King Day, Presidents Day,

    Labor Day, Veterans Day, Thanksgiving Day and Christmas

The Edwards Mansion: Closed for Renovation

    700 North 4th Street, Springfield, 62702

    (217) 523-2631; donation requested

    Mary Todd's sister was related to the owners of this mansion

    On display is a couch used by Lincoln to court Mary Todd

    SCHEDULED TO OPEN AGAIN FEBRUARY OF 2015

Henson Robinson Zoo:

    1100 E. Lake Shore Drive, Springfield, Il, 62712

    Telephone: (217) 585-1821

    Nov-Feb: 10m – 4pm but Jan & Feb open weekends only

    March–Oct: Mon-Fri: 10am–5pm; Sat-Sun: 10am-6pm

    Website: **www.hensonrobinsonzoo.org**

    Admission: Adults: $5.75; Seniors $4.25; Children (3-12): $4.00

    Children under 2: free; group rates for 10 or more;

    Closed: Thanksgiving& the day after; Christmas &New Years

Lincoln Herndon Law Offices: Closed for renovation

    Old State Capitol Plaza (6th and Adams), Springfield, IL 62701

    (217) 785-7289;

    Lincoln's former law office

    Not expected to be reopened until 2016; however, the Old State

    Capitol is open;

For additional attractions and for other hotels & restaurants, go to
www.visitspringfieldIllinois.com

THOMAS WOODROW WILSON

28th President 1913 – 1921

First Ladies:
Ellen Axson Wilson (died in 1914)
Edith Galt Wilson (married Wilson in 1915)

Thomas Woodrow Wilson was born in this stately home on December 28, 1856, five years before the start of the Civil War. The Presbyterian Church provided the home to Wilson's father who was its minister. It stands next to Wilson's museum and is open to the museum's visitors. The home and its furnishings have been restored to their original condition. The Wilson Home and Museum are located in the charming town of Staunton, Virginia, (Virginians pronounce it "Stan-ton") nestled in the beautiful Shenandoah Valley near the Blue Ridge Mountains of Virginia.

EARLY YEARS: When "Tommy" (as he was called as a child) was only a year old, his family left Staunton, Virginia because his father was offered a more lucrative position in the Deep South. The boy who would become our 28th President experienced the Civil War in Augusta, Georgia, where his father was the Minister of the First Presbyterian Church and where slavery was an accepted and fiercely defended practice. His "teen" years (14-18) were spent in Colombia, South Carolina. His childhood left him with a loathing of war but with a strong belief that segregation was _good_ for the country.

Wilson was a poor student until the age of ten and may have suffered from dyslexia. But once he taught himself to read, he did so voraciously. He was home-schooled until he entered a local college and, in 1875 he transferred to the College of New Jersey (its name changed to Princeton University in 1896). There he became active in political and literary debating societies and discovered that he was a persuasive public speaker.

GRADUATE STUDIES: Wilson is the only U.S. President to have earned a doctorate degree. After briefly practicing law, he applied to graduate school at Johns Hopkins University and earned his Ph.D. in history and political science in 1886. His doctoral thesis was entitled, _Congressional Government: A study in American Politics_ and it was the first of many academic papers in which he discussed possible government reforms.

PRINCETON: Wilson joined the Princeton faculty in 1890 and in 1902 he was promoted to President of the University, presumably because the trustees noticed his administrative talents. Wilson increased the prestige of Princeton University by hiring scholars and professors from top colleges, making public speeches about the University and raising Princeton's admission standards. Wilson had a mild stroke in 1896 that involved his arm. One day ten years later he found that he suddenly could not see out of one eye. Doctors told him to take time off from work, which he did for a few months, but was then back on the job. When he returned in 1906, he took on more stressful work than he had before. He tried to abolish school policies that tolerated special treatment for a subset of students that he called, "the spoiled sons of the wealthy." Wilson met fierce objection from the school board. He came to realize that his progressive ideas were never going to be adopted by the privileged men who made up much of

Princeton's governing body.

Although Wilson was losing his fight at Princeton, the contentious issues that he fought for were widely reported, and Wilson was praised in local newspapers. Political Party bosses took note of this publicity and promptly asked him to run as a progressive Democrat for Governor of New Jersey in 1910. He agreed but wanted to remain as President of Princeton if he didn't win the race. Instead, the trustees kicked him out, using the excuse that he was spending too much time campaigning.

AN ACADEMIC ENTERS POLITICS: Wilson won the race for Governor by a large margin. And then he promptly decreased the enormous power of Party bosses who had backed his candidacy by establishing New Jersey's first state primary elections. He supported and enacted several progressive State laws, such as worker's compensation for injury and disability. His popularity in New Jersey drew national attention and led him to be chosen as the Democratic candidate for President in 1912.

A PRESIDENT BENT ON REFORM: The presidential election of 1912 was a four-way race between: (1) Wilson, the progressive Democrat; (2) Eugene Debs, the Socialist Party candidate who felt that the government should own the large industries; (3) William Howard Taft, the incumbent Republican President who had continued Theodore Roosevelt's "trust-busting" activity; and (4) Teddy Roosevelt, the former Republican President who split the Republican vote by running on the Progressive or "Bull Moose" Party ticket. ("Bull Moose" was one of Theodore's many nicknames).

Wilson campaigned as a moderate progressive. He did not suggest adding significantly to the power of the Federal government (although he later did just that) but he promised to fight corruption. His "New Freedom" platform proposed to reform business practices, protect consumers and help farmers and small businesses to compete with growing conglomerates. Wilson's win may have been due to Roosevelt's splitting of the Republican vote. Woodrow Wilson became President of the United States on March 4, 1913.

INDUSTRIAL BOOM: U.S. industries were thriving. There was a growing middle class who lived comfortably, however a large portion of the population lived in poverty and endured harsh and unsafe working conditions.

Less than 1% of the population lived in luxury and could afford limousines like the shiny black 1919 Pierce Arrow shown above, which President Wilson received as a gift. The 1% was made up of people like John D Rockefeller who dominated the oil industry, Andrew Carnegie who dominated the steel industry and JP Morgan, a tycoon in banking and railroads.

Corruption was common, and many people were demanding reforms. Initially, Wilson didn't focus on his "New Freedom" platform.

Rather, he focused on three major areas: - *Tariff Reform* – which meant lowering tariffs to reduce the cost of imports to America; *Tax Reform* – which meant adding a personal income tax to raise revenue for the government; and *Banking Reform* – which meant creating the Federal Reserve System that allows the government to regulate the supply of money. Later he passed the Federal Farm Loan Act that gave farmers access to much needed credit, and business reform, which meant passing the Clayton Anti-Trust Act and the Federal Trade Act, which enabled the government to investigate illegal business practices and eliminate unfair business arrangements such as trusts and monopolies.

On the domestic front, the 18th amendment was ratified in Wilson's second term, prohibiting the manufacture, sale and transport of "intoxicating liqueurs."   Congress then passed the National Prohibition Act of 1919, known as the Volstead Act, which defined what the 18th amendment meant by the term, "intoxicating liqueurs" and provided strict penalties for violating the 18th amendment. Although Wilson vetoed the Volstead Act, Congress immediately overrode his veto with the result that criminal gangs gained enormous power. Prohibition was ended in 1933 during the Great Depression.

For years Wilson ignored women's demand for the right to vote; however, he finally relented in his second term and signed the 19th amendment, which was ratified by the states in 1920. That amendment made it illegal to deny the right to vote to any American citizen on the basis of sex. Unfortunately, people could still be denied that right on the basis of color.   Indeed, racial discrimination was sanctioned throughout the country, and Wilson, who had lived much of his life in the Deep South, actually increased segregation in the Federal government rather than trying to eliminate it.

THE GREAT WAR: World War I, or as it was called then, "The Great War," began in Europe on August 14, 1914, and President Wilson declared that the United States would remain neutral. Perhaps his memories of the Civil War in the South made him determined to stay out of what he considered to be "Europe's problems." For more than two years, Wilson maintained neutrality, although he secretly supplied weapons and ammunition to England and France. The mood of the country was decidedly isolationist and, when Wilson ran for re-election in 1917, he was hailed as the President who had maintained "Peace with Honor." Ironically, Wilson's selling military and other supplies to France and Britain helped to bring the U.S. economy out of its slump, and probably was a major factor in Wilson's reelection.

Two events in early 1917 changed the nation's mood and forced a reluctant Wilson to ask Congress for a Declaration of War. First, a secret telegram was intercepted by the British and leaked to the American public. It was sent in code from the German Foreign Minister in Berlin, Arthur Zimmermann, to the German Ambassador in Mexico. The famous "Zimmermann Telegram" inflamed the U.S. public by proposing that, if Mexico would stage an attack on the United States, not only would Germany reward it financially, but Mexico also would gain parts of Texas, New Mexico and Arizona. Although Mexico turned down this German proposal, the American public was enraged. The second turning point was Germany's sinking of American ships in the Atlantic, despite America's declared neutrality. The truth is that some American ships were carrying munitions to Germany's enemies, which undermined the U.S. claim to neutrality. Although Americans turned in favor of entering the war, they were not prepared for Wilson's next step. To everyone's surprise, Wilson began drafting soldiers rather than relying on a voluntary army.

TRENCH WARFARE: One of the Wilson Museum's most gripping exhibits about World War I is a full-scale reproduction of the trenches that had been built along hundreds of miles of the front lines of battle. Trench warfare was a horrific slaughter of soldiers by deadly hand-grenades and canisters of mustard gas that continued month after month along the stationary line of trenches with neither side gaining ground. Even with the arrival of U.S. troops, the carnage of trench warfare continued for more than a year.

PEACE TREATY: When the two sides finally conceded they couldn't win the war militarily, they sent representatives to *Versailles, France* to negotiate a peace treaty. Wilson proposed "fourteen points" that he hoped would cause Europeans to live in peace. Our European allies eliminated most of Wilson's points and replaced them with harsh demands on Germany.   However, the Europeans did adopt his last point, which established a League of Nations. This became part of the armistice signed by all parties on November 11, 1918. Wilson hoped that The Great War would be the last European war and that, in the future, countries would settle problems diplomatically. He wanted the League of Nations to be his legacy.

FIGHT FOR THE LEAUGE OF NATIONS: Unfortunately, Wilson was not on good terms with the leaders of the Republican Party in the Senate, especially the Senate Leader, Henry Cabot Lodge. Wilson had refused to allow any Republican leaders to accompany him to the Versailles negotiations. The result was what one would expect; the Senate Republicans refused to ratify the treaty until changes they wanted were made, including major revisions to the provision regarding the League of Nations. Wilson knew that it would be difficult if not impossible for Europe to change a multinational treaty that had taken months of negotiation to finalize.

Wilson appealed to the American people to put pressure on the Senate to sign the existing treaty and he went on a nationwide tour advocating for the League of Nations.   During this grueling trip he became ill and his doctor insisted that he return to the White House for a rest. Almost immediately on his return, President Wilson suffered a massive stroke that partially paralyzed his left side and almost killed him. As a result, his hopes that the U.S. would join the League of Nations were dashed.

The Versailles Treaty was not ratified. Senate Democrats who were loyal to Wilson refused to accept any Republican proposals to change the Treaty and the U.S., therefore, did not join the League of Nations. The Republicans won a landslide victory in 1920 by denouncing Wilson's policies. Under the next President, Warren Harding, Congress ratified a modified U.S.–German Peace Treaty that kept the U.S. out of the League of Nations, which was finally signed in Berlin in August 1921.

LAST YEAR OF WILSON'S PRESIDENTCY: Incredibly, Wilson's disabling stroke was kept secret from the public, and even from most politicians. Wilson was not heard from during the last year of his Presidency and his wife, Edith Galt Wilson, was literally the acting President of the United States. She decided what was important enough for her husband to see and what legislation he should sign.

END OF THE LEAGUE OF NATIONS: Without U.S. support, the League of Nations struggled in vain to remain relevant for several years. When it failed to prevent World War II, it was dissolved and its headquarters in Geneva Switzerland were abandoned.

Six years later, in 1945, that building became an office of the United Nations with the strong support of the United States.

LESSONS LEARNED: One leaves the Wilson Museum wondering why a man with distaste for war sent U.S. troops into the "European" war. George Washington may have been rolling over in his grave when Wilson took sides in a foreign war in which the clear interests of the U.S. were not at stake. Even Wilson recognized that this European conflict posed no threat to the United Sates. Germany only attacked ships suspected of carrying military supplies to its enemies, which the U.S. ships were in fact secretly doing.

Looking back, Wilson may have entered the war because he held a strong belief that was later expressed by John F. Kennedy, who said in 1963, "mankind must do away with war or war will do away with mankind."[2] Wilson may have taken part in order to influence how peace in Europe would be achieved. Wilson sincerely wanted World War I to be "the war to end all wars" and he died trying unsuccessfully to help keep the peace by bringing the U.S. into the League of Nations. Unfortunately, he also failed in his effort to prevent the winners from severely punishing the losers of that war. Germany was forced to pay huge reparations and submit to other punitive actions as well. The harsh treatment of Germany by the Versailles Treaty is thought to be the reason that Hitler was able to take over the leadership of a humiliated country eager to restore its pride.

WILSON'S LEGACY: During the eight tumultuous years of Wilson's presidency, a growing middle class got many of the reforms

[2] Kennedy, J,, *American University Speech,* June 10, 1963.

they had demanded. The economy and the stature of the United States on the world stage grew as well. And the dreadful memories of The Great War resulted in a return to isolationism.

AUTHRORS' NOTE: The Wilson Museum in Staunton is not the only Woodrow Wilson museum. Two others that we know about are the house where he lived in Washington, DC for three years after his Presidency, and his family's home in Columbia, South Carolina. We chose to visit the Staunton museum because it was close to other museums that we planned to visit. It turned out that Staunton is a wonderful town with a great Shakespeare theatre.

Visiting Woodrow Wilson's Presidential Museum

20 N. Coalter Street, Staunton, VA, 24401

(540) 885-0897; Website: www.woodrowwilson.org

Museum Hours:

Mon-Sat: 9am-5pm; Closed Tues and Wed in Jan & Feb
Sunday: 12noon-5pm
Closed Easter, Thanksgiving, Christmas and New Year's Day

Museum Admission Fees:

$14 Adults (14-61)
$12 Seniors (62+), Active military and AAA members
$7 Students (13+)
$5 Children (6-12); No charge for children under age 6

Tour of Wilson's House:

Museum Admission Fees noted above include a guided tour of Wilson's home (which is next door to the Museum) at the following times: 10am, 11am, 12:15pm, 1:30pm, 2:45pm and 4pm.

Where to Purchase Tickets:

Purchase tickets at the Museum's gift store counter or on the Museum's website; Tickets are not date specific so they are refundable; however, refunds are only made at the Museum, and not online.

Adult Groups:

Adult groups of at least 10 people are eligible for a discounted admission Fee of $8 per person if they reserve in advance. Please contact Cynthia Polhill at (540) 885-0897, ext. 106 or email her at **cpolhill@woodrowwilson.org**.'

Private Tours

The Museum offers several different private tours that require advance registration. To find out what these are, please contact

Cynthia Polhill at the number or email provided above.

Parking

Parking is free for Museum visitors; drive past the Museum and turn left onto East Frederick Street; go ½ way down the block and go left into the Museum's parking lot. .

Accessibility

There is no wheelchair access from the parking lot to the Museum; however, there is one handicap space for a car on the side of the Museum; Turn into the Museum's driveway and drive to the back of the Museum. It's on the left.

Suggestions for Lodging:

Frederick House (Bed & Breakfast)

28 North New Street, Staunton, VA 24401

(540) 885-4220; Website: **www.frederickhouse.com**

Free wi-fi; free breakfast; free parking; no pets

Children 6 & older welcome; Shakespeare and other "packages"

The Stonewall Jackson Hotel and Conference Center

Address: 24 S. Market Street, Staunton, VA 24401

(540) 885-4848; Website: **www.stonewalljacksonhotel.com**

Indoor Pool, free wi-fi; pets allowed ($50 fee); paid public parking

Hampton Inn

40 Payne Lane, Staunton, VA 24401

(540) 886-7000; Website: **www.hamptoninn3.hilton.com**

Free breakfast, free parking, free wi-fi; no pets;

Suggestions for Restaurants:

Aioli – Mediterranean & Tapas

29 N. Augusta Street, Staunton, VA 24401

(540) 885-1414; Website: **www.aiolistaunton.com**

Tues-Thu: 5pm–9:30pm; Fri-Sat: 5:00 pm–10pm

Byers Street Bistro – American

18 Byers Street, Staunton, VA 24401

(540) 887-6100; Website: **www.byersstreetbistro.com**

Mon-Sun: 11am – Midnight;

Mill Street Grill
1 Mill Street in Staunton, VA 24401
(540) 886-0656; Website: **www.millstreetgrill.com**
Mon-Thu: 4pm-10pm; Fri-Sat: 4:00pm-10:30pm
Sunday: 11am-9:30pm; No reservations

Pampered Palate Cafe – sandwiches
26 E. Beverley Street, Staunton, VA 24401
(540) 886-9463; Website: **www.thepamperedpalatecafe.com**
Mon-Thu: 9am – 4:30pm; Fri: 9am–7:30pm
Sat 9am–5:30pm; Closed Sunday and a week in Jan and Sept

The Depot Grill – American
42 Middlebrook Ave, Staunton, VA 24401
(540) 885-7332; Website: **www.depotgrille.com**
Mon-Thu: 11am–9pm; Fri-Sat: 11am-10pm
Closing hours vary between 9pm and 10:30pm
Free parking lots front and back

Attractions in Staunton:

Staunton Augusta Art Center:
Exhibitions are in the R.R. Smith Center for History & Art
20 S. New Street, Staunton, VA 24401
(540) 885-2028; No admission charge
Mon-Fri: 10am-5pm; Sat: 10am-4pm. Closed on Sundays
Paid parking across the street in a public garage

Blackfriars Playhouse: <u>Live Shakespeare Performances</u>
>Address: 10 South Market Street, Staunton, VA 24401
>Box Office Number: (877) 682-4236; 10% off for AAA;
>Box office is open Monday–Saturday: 9:30am–6pm;
>also open for only "walk-ins" one hour prior to performance
>Tickets are usually in demand, so you might want to buy tickets in advance by phone or online at:
>**www.AmericanShakespeareCenter.com**
>Note: No AAA discounts are given online
>ALL TICKETS ARE NONREFUNDABLE so double check in advance to see if you might be able to use them at a different performance if your trip schedule changes

Frontier Culture Museum:
>An outdoor museum with exhibits on early immigrants to America including farmhouses, colonial houses and a school
>1290 Richmond Road, Staunton, VA 24401
>(540) 332-7850; Website: **www.Frontiermuseum.org**
>Open 7 days a week. Closed on state holidays including Thanksgiving Day, Christmas Day and New Years Day
>Mid-March -November 30: 9am-5pm
>December 1-Mid-March: 10am-4pm
>$10 Adult; $9.50 Senior; $9 Student (13-college); $6 Child (6-12)
>Children under age 6 are free;

Gypsy Hill Park. It has 214 acres for family fun: public swimming pool, picnic tables, tennis courts, duck ponds and playgrounds
>600 Churchville Ave, Staunton
>Telephone: (540) 332-3945
> Hours: Monday-Sunday: 6am until 11pm

Note: Go to **www.visitstaunton.com** and click on "Events" to find out what else is happening in Staunton on the dates of your visit.

HERBERT HOOVER

31st President 1929 – 1933

First Lady: Lou Henry Hoover

The Herbert Hoover Museum tells a powerful story that few people know. Many think of President Hoover as the president who caused the Great Depression. He has been cast as a man who knew nothing about poverty and cared little about the poor. A visit to the Hoover Museum just outside of vibrant Iowa City shows how wrong each of those notions is. Although Hoover was wealthy by the time he entered politics, he never took a salary for his public service and used his own money to provide relief and rescue for people around the world.

FROM POOR ORPHAN TO SELF-MADE MILLIONAIRE: Herbert Hoover was born in the small house pictured above in West Branch, Iowa, on what is now a lovely park surrounding his museum. His father was a blacksmith and died when Herbert was six. His mother died three years later. At the age of ten he was sent to live with an Uncle in Oregon whom he had never met. He was separated from his brother and sister because no one in his family could afford to take care of all three siblings.

Young Hoover, like many would-be presidents, had a love of books; but he had no formal schooling until the age of eighteen. After two attempts, he passed the entrance exam for the brand new Stanford University in Palo Alto California, which offered one year's free tuition to its first class of students. Hoover raised the rest of his tuition working odd jobs, and earned a degree in geology in 1895. He was immediately hired by a gold-mining company and was sent to Western Australia, which he described in a letter at the Museum as a land of "black flies, red dust and white heat."

At the age of 23, Hoover was appointed as mine manager and was soon offered another promotion to head up mining operations in China. Financially secure, he returned briefly to the United States, married his Stanford sweetheart, Lou Henry, and the two of them promptly headed off to China. While developing mines in rural China, he helped to end the long-term servitude contracts of Chinese workers and instituted reforms to improve their working conditions and pay. Hoover was a multi-millionaire by the time he was 40. He had worked in the most uninviting corners of the globe and had become one of the world's best mining engineers with offices in several of the world's major cities. In his spare time, he wrote and lectured. His 1909 book, *Principles of Mining*, became a standard textbook.

PATRIOT AND PHILANTHROPIST: Hoover was in London at the outbreak of the First World War on August 14, 1914, and that day changed his life, igniting his patriotism and calling him to public service. He began by using his own money and that donated by his friends to provide food, assistance and steam ship tickets home for the many Americans trapped in Europe. He then sent massive amounts of aid to Belgian civilians who were starving in the wake of the German invasion. President Wilson learned of Hoover's humanitarian efforts and, in 1917, appointed him to head the U.S. Food Administration, providing food to allies during the war, and relief and reconstruction after the war ended.

Hoover did not only set up relief efforts for people living in countries that were allied with the U.S. He used his own money and raised private funds to send food to starving people in the enemy territories of Germany and Austria. In 1921, a famine was causing mass starvation in the midst of the Russian civil war. President Warren Harding had offered Russia an aid package in return for the release of American prisoners of war (Americans had participated in attempts to overthrow the Bolshevik government). When the Bolsheviks refused to allow Americans to distribute the aid, the President asked Hoover to intervene. Despite widespread famine, a deadly outbreak of typhus and the raging Russian civil war, Hoover went to Russia. He successfully negotiated with the Red Army and was able to establish and oversee a massive relief program. His program saved millions of lives, and won the release of American prisoners.

THE BUSINESS OF GOVERNMENT: After returning to the United States, Hoover was appointed Secretary of Commerce under President Harding and continued in that position under President Calvin Collidge. Hoover transformed that little-used agency into one that would permanently change the nation. Newly invented products that were flooding the marketplace improved lives, but they were also causing chaos because of their lack of uniform standards. Hoover standardized the sizes of bricks, plumbing and electrical fixtures so that they would fit in any home. He saw to it that tires would fit more than one brand of car and milk containers would hold pints, and quarts rather than arbitrary volumes. His streamlining of manufacturing, commerce, construction and transportation spurred the booming 1920s economy.

In 1927 Hoover was called upon to respond to another crisis. The historic Mississippi River flood of 1927 was devastating. An area 50 miles wide and 100 miles long was inundated with 30 feet of water, causing death, destruction and the displacement of large populations. President Coolidge sent his Secretary of Commerce into action. Once more Hoover demonstrated his skill at organizing a major relief effort. He worked with state and local officials and mobilized an army of volunteers. Hoover's team brought supplies to the area with hundreds of ships, built tent cities and raised millions of dollars for the Red Cross.

HOOVER AS PRESIDENT: In 1928 Hoover campaigned for the Presidency and won easily, becoming our 31st President in 1929. At his inauguration, Hoover warned the nation he was not *"a superman."* If some unprecedented calamity should come along during his Presidency, he didn't want people to expect miracles. Looking back on that speech, it's as if Hoover had a crystal ball. Only eight months later the stock market crashed and, despite his best efforts, the Great Depression had begun. Even though only a small percentage of the population owned stocks at that time, the entire economy spun into total collapse.

As the economic slide continued to worsen, Hoover took the

unprecedented step of starting Federal public works projects. Before this, the states and local communities had always been the ones to take responsibility for infrastructure projects in their areas. In order to try to stimulate the economy, Hoover ordered the Federal construction of a hydroelectric dam across the Colorado River that would later bear his name. He also ordered several other Federal construction projects, such as the Bay Bridge between San Francisco and Oakland, and two impressive buildings in Washington D.C., the U.S. Supreme Court Building and the National Archives Building. In addition, Hoover established the Reconstruction Finance Corporation that gave billions in aid to local governments and made loans to businesses.

U.S. Supreme Court Building
Washington, D.C

National Archives Building
Washington, D.C

However, Hoover definitely made mistakes, which are told in the Museum's exhibits. For example, President Hoover signed into law a bill to raise Federal revenue, which increased taxes on Corporations as well as individuals. This had the effect of weakening the struggling economy. Against the advice of many economists, Hoover also signed into law the Smoot-Haley Tariff Act that raised tariffs on imported goods to cause Americans to purchase cheaper products made in the U.S. This backfired because other nations retaliated by raising tariffs on U.S. goods sold in their countries, thereby causing a decline in U.S. exports. Counted among Hoover's worst mistakes was the treatment of his administration toward veterans of the Great War who marched on

Washington to collect bonuses that were supposed to be paid to them in 1945. However, this was only 1932, and the Senate had voted down a bill to pay the bonuses early. This group of veterans came to be known as the Bonus Army. They set up a large camp across the river from the Capitol and when they crossed over and began protesting near the Capitol, the local police tried to get them to stop.

Fights broke out and Hoover called on General MacArthur to move the veterans back to their camp. Unfortunately, MacArthur ignored Hoover's instructions and instead had his troops charge the veterans with fixed bayonets and destroyed their camp forcing them to leave town. Hoover took the blame for this, and it appeared to the American people that Hoover didn't care about the poor.

The "Bonus Army" Camp after Gen. MacArthur's attack

The election of 1932 was an easy contest for President Hoover's opponent, Democratic candidate, Franklin Roosevelt (FDR). Hoover was unpopular for so many reasons, including the fact that he could not bring himself to provide direct Federal relief to starving Americans, and also because he was a poor communicator who failed to lift up the spirits of the American people in a time of crisis. Although many homes had radios by then, Hoover did not take advantage of that medium. FDR was elected in a landslide because he blamed Hoover for the Depression, revealingly calling it "Hoover's Depression" while reminding his audience of how he (FDR) had acted boldly as Governor of New York to provide relief when the stock market crashed.

As Herbert Hoover left office, his name became a symbol of the Great Depression. However, he did not end his service to the United States when he left the White House. He answered President Truman's call to help with the enormous relief efforts necessary in Europe after World War II. Truman also appointed Hoover to head a commission to find ways to downsize government and to make it more efficient. President Eisenhower set up a similar commission, also with Hoover at the helm. When Herbert Hoover was 88 years old, he attended the opening of the Hoover Presidential Museum with Harry Truman at his side. He passed away two years later, and was buried outside the Museum alongside his wife, Lou.

One of the most disturbing things we learned during our visit to the Herbert Hoover Presidential Museum relates to the interim period between FDR's winning the election in November 1932 and FDR's inauguration in March of 1933. (Presidential inaugurations did not occur on January 20th until 1937 with the passage of the 20th Amendment) Hoover was a "lame duck" President for four full months after Roosevelt's election while the economy was shrinking fast. Unfortunately, the two men were unable to agree on any actions during this period and neither was willing to take unilateral action. The inability of these men to work together caused the banking crisis to deepen. Hoover appealed to FDR to jointly declare a bank holiday and call for a special session of Congress to fix the problems with the banks. FDR refused.

The FDR Museum, which we will visit next, displays this photograph of Hoover accompanying Roosevelt to the Inauguration ceremonies on March 4th, 1933. The caption reads: *"By Inauguration Day, the two were barely on speaking terms. Riding to the Capitol, Hoover sat expressionless while Roosevelt smiled and waved to the crowd. After March 4th, they never met again."*

Visiting Herbert Hoover's Presidential Museum

210 Parkside Drive West Branch, Iowa 52358

(319) 643-5301; Website: www.hoover.archives.gov

Museum Hours:
> Mon-Sun: 9am-5pm
> Closed Thanksgiving, Christmas Day and New Year's Day

Museum Admission Fees:
> $6 Adult (16-61); $3 Senior (62+); Children 15 and under are free
> Although decisions on pricing have not yet been made for 2015, admission fees for this museum will definitely increase

Group Tours:
> Call (319) 643-6031 for Tour information & registration.
> Groups of 15 or more can call ahead to schedule a guided tour

Student Groups:
> Teacher and students are free; One chaperone for every 10 students gets free admission; no discount for other chaperones
> Call the Museum to arrange your school tour

Home School:
> Free admission for one adult per family with advance registration.

Parking: There is a free parking lot at the Museum;

Special Needs: The Museum has several wheelchairs available on a first come basis.

Suggestions for Lodging

Hampton Inn Iowa City/University Area
> 4 Sturgis Corner Dr., Iowa City, IA 52240
> (319) 339-8000; Website: **www.iowacityia.hamptoninn.com**
> Indoor swimming pool, Free Wi-Fi, Free breakfast, Free parking
> No Pets.

Clarion highlander Hotel & Conference Center
> 2525 North Dodge Street, Iowa City, IA 52245
> (319) 354-2000 or (800) 424-6423
> Pets allowed ($20 fee per night). Six smoking rooms
> Indoor swimming pool, Free Wi-Fi, Free breakfast, Free parking
> Hotel website: **www.clarionhighlander.com**

Homewood Suites by Hilton Coralville - Iowa River Landing
> 921 E. 2nd Avenue, Coralville, IA 52241
> (319) 338-3410; Website: **www.homewoodsuites.com**
> Indoor swimming pool, Free Wi-Fi, Free breakfast
> No pets; free parking

Brown Street Inn Bed & Breakfast
> 430 Brown Street, Iowa City, IA 52245
> (319) 338-0435; Website: **www.brownstreetinn.com**
> No pets: Children 12 and older are welcome;
> Free parking, free Wi-Fi, free breakfast
> Five bedrooms and one suite, all with private baths

A Bella Vista Bed & Breakfast
> 2 Bella Vista Pl., Iowa City, IA 52245
> (319) 338-4129; Website: **www.abellavista.net**
> Children age 7 and older are welcome
> Free Wi-Fi, Free breakfast, Free parking; No pets
> Three rooms with private baths; two rooms with shared bath

Smiths' Bed & Breakfast
> 314 Brown Street, Iowa City, IA 52245
> (319) 338-1316; Children of all ages are welcome
> Free parking, free Wi-Fi, free breakfast; no pets
> Three bedrooms: one with bath and two that share a bath

Suggestions for Restaurants

Atlas World Grill (Mix of American & other country's dishes)
> 127 Iowa Ave, Iowa city, IA 52240
> (319) 341-7700; Website: **www.atlasiowacity.com**
> Hours: Monday – Sunday: 11am – 10pm

Baroncini Restorante (Italian)

> 104 S. Linn Street, Iowa city, IA 52240
> (319) 337-2048; Website: **www.baroncinirestaurant.com**
> Lunch: Monday – Friday: 11:30 am – 2pm
> Dinner: Monday – Saturday: 5:30 pm – 10pm

Linn Street Café (American)

> 121 N. Linn Street, Iowa city, IA 52245
> (319) 337-7370; Website: **www.linnstreetcafe.com**
> Dinner only; Mon–Thu: 5pm–9pm; Fri-Sat: 5pm–10pm

One Twenty Six (French American Bistro)

> 126 East Washington Street, Iowa city, IA 52240
> (319) 887-1909: Website: **www.onetwentysix.net**
> Lunch: Mon-Sat: 11am–2pm; Dinner: 5pm–9:30pm:
> Dinner every day of the week: 5pm–9:30pm
> Summer weekend dinner hours: 5pm–10pm

Hamburg Inn #2 (American)

> 214 N. Linn Street, Iowa city, IA 52245
> (319) 337-5512; Website: **www.hamburginn.com**
> 7 days a week: 6:30am–11pm

Attractions in the Area

Riverside Theatre

> 213 North Gilbert Street, Iowa City, 52245
> (319) 887-1360; Website: **www.riversidetheatre.org**
> A professional theatre that produces classic & new plays plus musicals and comedy shows all year round; -
> Tickets: Buy online at the Theatre's website or call their Box Office at **(319) 338-7672** Mon-Fri: 12noon to 4pm; or go to the Box Office in person: **213 N. Gilbert Street, Iowa City** between 12noon and 4pm Mon-Fri, or one hour before a show

Hancher Performances (affiliated with the University of Iowa)

This is a professional dance, music and theater group that lost its theatre in 2008 due to a major flood in Iowa City. They continue to perform in various places around town and probably will have a new building in 2016.

Tickets for Hancher Performances: You can check their schedule and buy tickets on their website: **hancher.uiowa.edu**, or call the Box Office **(319) 335-1160 Mon-Fri, 10am-5:30-pm.** You may also buy them in person at their Box Office located in the Old Capitol Mall (University Capitol Centre), on the first floor at the south end by the parking ramp, next to Sweets & Treats. Hours: Mon-Fri: 10am–5:30pm; Parking is available in the Capitol Street Garage (220 S Capitol St) - the first hour is free.

Englent Theatre

221 E. Washington Street, Iowa City 52240 (319) 688-2653; Website: **www.englert.org**. This is a professional group that brings in shows from around the world as well as locally. You can buy tickets online, by phone or at the Box Office: Mon-Fri: 12noon to 6pm at the address above.

University of Iowa Museum of Art

1375 Highway 1, Iowa City 52246; Phone: (319) 335-1727; Website: **www.uima.uiowa.edu;** Unfortunately the museum's building was destroyed in the 2008 Iowa City flood, but their fantastic collection of art was saved; see the Website for their exhibitions in temporary quarters and watch for the announcement of their new home. Admission is free.

Museum of Natural History

17 North Clinton Street, Iowa City 52240 (Located in Macbride Hall on University of Iowa Campus); Phone: (319) 335-0480; Website: **www.uiowa.edu/mnh**. Admission is free; Hours: Tue-Wed & Fri-Sun: 10am–5pm; Thursday:10am-8pm If you would like a free tour, call (319) 335-2010; Closed Mondays and national holidays

FRANKLIN D. ROOSEVELT

32nd President – 1933-1945

First Lady: Eleanor Roosevelt

The Franklin Roosevelt Library and Museum is located on the East bank of the Hudson River in Hyde Park, New York.

This area is breathtakingly beautiful at any time of the year, but especially so in the fall. We visited as the leaves were beginning to show their spectacular autumn colors. President Roosevelt designed his own library/museum, raised the money to build it, and is the only President who actually worked in his library while still in office. The Museum, which was renovated in 2013, is located on property that belonged to President Roosevelt's family.

HAPPY DAYS ARE HERE AGAIN: This was FDR's campaign song during a particularly unhappy period of the nation's history. When he was sworn in as President in 1933, FDR appeared to be exactly what the country needed in those troubled times: a cheerful man of action. Optimism was the essence of FDR's personality despite the fact that he had been paralyzed from the waist down since 1921 when, at the age of 39, he contracted polio.

EARLY POLITICS: Prior to his paralysis in 1921, FDR had been a vigorous young man, a consummate politician and a rising star in political circles. He began by representing his Hyde Park district in the New York State Senate. FDR had always admired his older cousin, former President Theodore Roosevelt, and hoped that he would some day follow in his footsteps. When FDR accepted President Wilson's appointment as Assistant Secretary of the Navy, he was doing just that. His cousin Teddy had held that same job in his early days of politics, and FDR aspired to follow Teddy's path to the top job, the Presidency. In 1920, FDR was chosen to be the Democratic Vice-Presidential nominee on the ticket that lost to Republican Warren Harding; however, when he contracted polio in 1921, many thought his political career was over.

FDR'S DISABILITY: Each morning FDR had to be helped out of bed and into a wheelchair. When he was seen walking in public, it was only for a few steps at a time, and only because of heavy leg braces that he put on each morning and the support provided by the arm of a strong companion and/or a cane at his side. To make a speech he needed to grip a podium that had been bolted to the floor.

RE-ENTRY INTO POLITICS: FDR was determined to return to politics despite his disability, and he had strong encouragement from his wife, Eleanor Roosevelt (E.R.). His opportunity came in 1928, when he was nominated and elected Governor of New York State. By the time he ran for President in 1932, most people knew him as the "progressive" Governor of New York. He held the view, considered radical by many, that government should provide "relief" (as aid was called in those days), *not as a matter of charity, but as a matter of social duty.*[3] In 1931, under Governor Roosevelt, New York became the first State to provide assistance to the unemployed.[4] Based on what he had done for New Yorkers, many Americans believed that as their President, FDR would provide the relief that so many Americans desperately needed. What they wanted was a President who would take bold, immediate action and knew how to clearly communicate his plans to the people.

---

[3] Kennedy, D., Freedom from Fear, (New York: Oxford University Press) 1999. p. 90.

[4] Hopkins, J., Ph.D., *The Social Welfare History Project: The New York State Temporary Emergency Relief Administration*: Oct 1, 1931. http://www.socialwelfarehistory.com/eras/temporary-emergency-relief-administration/

WINNING THE PRESIDENCY: FDR won the 1932 Presidential election with a decisive victory that brought with it comfortable Democratic majorities in both houses of Congress. However, FDR could not count on the conservative Southern Democrats going along with his New Deal program. To try to ensure compliance with his agenda, *"Roosevelt calculatingly withheld the distribution of some one hundred thousand patronage jobs to deserving Democrats until after the special legislative session that he had requested to convene on March 9, 1933, had adjourned."*[5]

COLLAPSE OF THE FINANCIAL SYSTEM: FDR's air of confidence was contagious and Americans took to heart the memorable line in his inaugural address, *"The only thing we have to fear is fear itself!"* And yet, there was a great deal to fear on that day. During the three years prior to FDR's inauguration, *"more than 5,000 banks had closed their doors and nine million savings accounts had vanished."*[6] During February 1933, shortly before FDR's March 4th inauguration, rumors started circulating that some banks, which had previously been perceived as sound, were about to go under. Frightened depositors rushed to withdraw their funds. Since deposits were not insured at that time (that would not be instituted until June of 1933), depositors could lose all of their money.

---

[5] Kennedy, D., Freedom from Fear, ,New York: Oxford University Press) 1999. pp. 129-130.
[6] Leuchtenburg, W. et al, The LIFE History of the United States vol. 11: The New Deal and War/1933-1945 (NY: Time Life Books) 1964. p. 10.

"Bank Run," 1933

The previous photograph shows a "run" on a bank, a dramatic result of the fear that Roosevelt spoke of. Scenes like this were taking place all around the country. People who had planned to ride out the depression with the money they had saved now wondered how they would survive if they didn't withdraw their money before their bank collapsed. By the day of FDR's inauguration, most banks had closed either because they had run low on cash or because they were ordered to close by their state's governor.

A "NEW DEAL:" President Roosevelt immediately called for a Bank Holiday, which Hoover had been proposing prior to the inauguration. On March 12th, in his first radio talk with the nation (these became known as "fireside chats") the President described why he had closed the banks, how he would reopen them as soon as they were found to be sound, and why the nation should be comfortable with his actions. He explained that the Treasury Department was evaluating every bank in the country that had not been liquidated. Those banks that passed this inspection would be allowed to reopen on a schedule that FDR spelled out during this first fireside chat.

Most households already had radios, but they were still a prized possession. Their polished wood cabinets and glowing dials made them the centerpiece of any room. People gathered to listen to FDR's reassuring fireside chats in rooms much like the Museum's replica of a

1930s kitchen, shown in the photo below.

At this exhibit visitors can listen to FDR's fireside chats and imagine their effect during the depression. These eagerly anticipated messages brought hope and caused many to view the President as a family friend. Some, however, remained bitterly opposed to his expanded view of the role of the federal government.

The new President quickly called Congress into session and presented them with proposals known as the "New Deal." He made his position clear. He demanded quick passage and threatened emergency powers if Congress failed to act. He said that his job of saving the economy and getting people back to work was like fighting a war. The country wanted quick action and they got it; not only from the President, but from a bi-partisan Congress anxious to lift up the economy. Congress convened on March 9, 1933, to vote on FDR's Emergency Banking Bill. Henry Steagall, the Chairman of the House Banking and Currency Committee described for the House members what they were being asked to pass. It took them less than an hour to pass a bill that they had not even seen in writing. The Senate took up the bill immediately; and that night the President signed the emergency Banking bill into law.

During the first one hundred days of his term, FDR sent a series of bills to Congress (including a bill to end the prohibition on beer). All of them were passed.[7] The bills included the following:

---

[7] Kennedy, D., Freedom from Fear, (New York: Oxford University Press) 1999.. pp 131-159.

March 9:	Emergency Banking Act
March 20:	Economy Act
March 31:	Civilian Conservation Corps (CCC)
April 19:	Gold Standard abandoned (ratified June 5)
May 12:	Federal Emergency Relief Act
May 12:	Agricultural Adjustment Act (AAA)
May 12:	Emergency Farm Mortgage Act
May 18:	Tennessee Valley Authority Act
May 27:	Federal-Securities Act
June 13:	Home Owner's Loan Act
June 16:	Glass-Steagall Banking Act
June 16:	Farm Credit Act
June 16	The National Industrial Recovery Act (NIRA)

The Civilian Conservation Corps (CCC), the Public Works Administration (WPA) and other New Deal agencies put millions of people back to work. According to museum documents, these programs created 12 million acres of national parks and forests, built over 625,000 miles of badly needed roads, over 4,000 modern airport buildings and more than 7 million feet of runways for a new commercial airline industry. Construction was begun on dams, bridges, schools and hospitals across the country. The Tennessee Valley Authority (TVA) brought hydroelectric power to Tennessee and the Rural Electrical Administration (REA) extended electrical service to rural areas throughout the nation.

The Banking Act of 1933 (also known as the Glass-Steagall Act) created the Federal Deposit Insurance Corporation (FDIC), which insured individual deposit accounts up to $5,000 (later raised) in banks that invested depositors' money in conservative investments. These were sometimes referred to as "commercial banks." The FDIC did not insure financial institutions that made risky bets with depositors' money because it was thought that taxpayers should not pay for gambling (today, such risky bets *are* insured). Banks that "gambled" were referred to as "investment banks" or more recently, "hedge funds." The important point is that the Banking Act made people more comfortable about putting their money in commercial banks because the FDIC would reimburse them if their bank went under. This helped to prevent "runs" on banks.

Farming legislation gave subsidies to farmers who had been suffering even before the 1929 stock market crash. Eleanor Roosevelt disliked this legislation because *"it benefited only large farm owners and never 'trickled down' to farm workers."*[8] The subsidies were supposed to be temporary.[9] However some still exist today, possibly because several members of Congress who themselves receive farm subsidies are permitted to sit on the committee that votes on whether those subsidies continue, and/or because some members of Congress have donors who are recipients of those farm subsidies and, since campaigns for reelection are so expensive, they need to keep their donors happy.

FDR was the first President to appoint a woman to a Cabinet position. Frances Perkins was named Secretary of Labor, and she successfully pressed for labor laws providing for minimum wages, maximum hours and the right of workers to form unions. She also pushed for Social Security, which was adopted in 1935. FDR did not go far enough for some, including the flamboyant, populist Senator from Louisiana, Huey P. Long. Others felt, however, that FDR's New Deal was a step in the wrong direction either because they believed government spending would stifle rather than grow the economy, or because they feared that FDR would turn the United States into a country like Bolshevik Russia as a result of his "socialist reforms." One thing is certain: FDR's programs in the 1930s indelibly changed the way we live, and they continue to provide a safety net for the retired, the sick, the disabled and the unemployed.

FIRST LADY AS ACTIVE PARTNER: FDR had another big advantage when he took office (in addition to being a great communicator and a bold thinker and doer with uncommon self-confidence). He had Eleanor Roosevelt (E.R.) as an energetic and intelligent partner who took on much more than the normal duties of a First Lady.

FDR considered E.R. to be his eyes and ears. She traveled around the country and later around the world telling him where the trouble spots were and letting him know whether or not his programs were

---

[8] Cook, B., Eleanor Roosevelt vol. 2: 1933-1938 (NY: Penguin Group) 1999. p. 81.
[9] Leuchtenburg, W. et al, The LIFE History of the United States vol. 11, The New Deal and War/1933-1945 (NY: Time Life Books) 1964., p. 12.

working. Rather than occupying a small section of the Museum, E.R.'s contributions to FDR's Presidency are seen in almost every section. There are exhibits showing what she did to advance the rights of women and to eliminate the unjust treatment of African-Americans. Another exhibit shows memos that E.R. sometimes placed in her husband's bedside reading basket, urging him to do what she believed needed most urgently to be done.[10] An example on display suggests that he should place a woman on the Home Loan Board, as seen below:

THE WHITE HOUSE: JANUARY 29, 1934

"What do you think about Marie Obenhaver who is a Republican to take the place on the Home Loan Board to fill the place of a Republican who is leaving it? She is very well fitted for this job. Please read the attached letter and give me an answer." She signed the Memo "E.R.". There are pencil notations on the memo added by the President after he read it.

When E.R. wasn't traveling around the country (which was often), she worked for diverse causes, writing a newspaper column, holding press conferences for women journalists and sometimes doing radio broadcasts, in addition to the normal job of a First Lady: hosting parties, greeting guests at the White House, etc. Later on E.R. agreed to write a nationally syndicated newspaper column called "My Day," which appeared six days a week. E.R. wrote some of her columns on this 1902, L.C. Smith typewriter that is now in the Museum.

On December 7th, 1941, immediately after the bombing of Pearl Harbor, while the President was meeting with his Cabinet, it was

[10] Cook, B., Eleanor Roosevelt vol. 2: 1933-1938 (NY: Penguin Group) 1999.. p. 31.

Eleanor Roosevelt who went on the radio to address the American people. With the firm voice that by then was familiar to the nation, she told them what happened and assured them that their government was working hard at that very minute to meet this challenge.

The First Lady also became directly involved when the "Bonus Army" reappeared in Washington, D.C. As we described in the previous chapter on Herbert Hoover, the "Bonus Army" consisted of World War I veterans who came to the capitol in 1932 to demand immediate payment of the bonus that Congress had authorized to be paid in 1945. They marched on Washington D.C. because they were out of work, out of money and in despair; however they were chased out of the city (against President Hoover's orders) by General MacArthur. Some of these veterans returned in 1933 and set up camp in Washington D.C. again, this time to appeal to President Roosevelt for an early payment. Although Congress was considering a bill to give them an early bonus, FDR was not in favor of it.

E.R. visited their camp and spent an hour talking with the veterans. Instead of finding "criminals" or "Communists" as some in the press had called them, E.R. found polite, wonderful people who were only concerned about the well being of their families. After Eleanor told FDR what she had seen, the President issued an executive order to allow these veterans to enroll in the Civilian Conservation Corps (CCC), even though they didn't meet all of CCC's qualifications. When asked about E.R.'s influence on FDR, Presidential Advisor, Rexford Tugwell, is quoted as saying, "*No one who ever saw Eleanor Roosevelt sit down facing her husband and, holding his eyes firmly, say to him, 'Franklin, I think you should'…or 'Franklin, surely you will not'…will ever forget the experience.*"

CIVIL RIGHTS FOR BLACKS: Mrs. Roosevelt was an early champion of civil rights for every downtrodden or unfairly treated American including African Americans. A famous example is on display at the FDR Museum: her letter of resignation from the Daughters of the American Revolution. That organization had refused to allow the "Negro" opera singer, Marian Anderson, to sing at Constitution Hall in Washington because of her race. After resigning, E.R. successfully urged Secretary of the Interior, Harold Ickes, to arrange for Ms. Anderson to give a nationally broadcast performance from the Lincoln Memorial. This historic concert was a poignant first step on a long journey that the country was reluctant to take. FDR was well aware of the political risk to his New Deal if he were to publicly support civil rights for blacks. He would surely lose the Southern Democrats' support for his New Deal proposals. For this reason, FDR did not permit black journalists to attend his press briefings, and he even refused to back a long overdue attempt to pass a federal anti-lynching law.

CAMPAIGNING FOR A SECOND TERM: FDR faced a tough campaign for re-election in 1936. Republicans nominated Alf Landon, the conservative Governor of Kansas, as their candidate for President. Many Republicans felt that the New Deal was stripping businessmen of their freedoms. FDR responded to this charge saying; *"Business leaders have begun to consider the government of the United States as a mere appendage to their own affairs. **We know that government by organized money is just as dangerous as government by organized mob"*** (emphasis added).[11] In fact, the economy had improved during FDR's first term, and it appears that many people must have been grateful for the New Deal reforms because FDR won an even bigger victory in 1936 than in 1932.

THE ROOSEVELT RECESSION: Between 1933 and 1937 unemployment dropped from 25% to 14.3% and the Gross National Product (GNP) was rising toward pre-Depression levels. The President thought the economy had turned the corner and that emergency spending was no longer necessary, especially because government spending in his first term produced a significant increase in the national debt. As a result, FDR tried to balance the budget in his second term by reducing government spending, including relief payments. The unfortunate result was that the economy went into a nosedive. 1937 and 1938 have been referred to as "the Roosevelt Recession." Although the economy was now much better than it had been at the depths of the Great Depression, it did not fully recover until the United States entered World War II, which ushered in an era of robust economic activity.

---

[11] Leuchtenburg, W. et al, The LIFE History of the United States vol. 11: The New Deal and War/1933-1945 (NY: Time Life Books,) 1964. pp. 56 & 57.

PACKING THE COURT: FDR made another huge mistake in his second term. He was furious that the Supreme Court had been overturning some of the New Deal reforms that had been put into law and he tried to prevent similar action by the Court on other New Deal reforms. He hatched a scheme that his accusers called "packing the court." He introduced a plan to increase the number of Justices on the Supreme Court so that he could appoint people who were favorably inclined towards the New Deal. This blatant political move was as unpopular with Democrats as it was with Republicans.

THE GATHERING STORM AND A THIRD TERM CAMPAIGN: In 1940 FDR was nominated for an unprecedented third term as President. Even though Hitler's forces already had brutally occupied much of Europe and were bombing London and sinking merchant ships in the Atlantic, the United States was in an isolationist mood, just as it had been for much of World War I. The Republican nominee, Wendell Willkie, was a well-known liberal businessman and a vocal internationalist. Now, even he began to court the votes of the large isolationist block of Republican voters who wanted above all else, to stay out of the European conflict. These included powerful people such as Joseph Kennedy, the Ambassador to Great Britain, and Charles Lindbergh the famous aviator. These men were unsympathetic to Hitler's victims and vehemently opposed to U.S. intervention. As the campaign got more intense, Willkie not only stopped advocating for intervention, he went so far as to claim that a third term with FDR would be disastrous because the President would plunge the U.S. into war.

FDR did not campaign much until just before the 1940 election. In her book, "1940," Susan Dunn writes, *"the president made the eminently rational and shrewd decision to stage himself as a nonpolitical commander in chief, dedicated to the defense of the nation, too occupied and preoccupied with matters of major importance to go out and plead for votes."* [12] Rather than actively "applying for the job," he merely increased his public visibility by meeting with important people and appearing at highly publicized events. This "Presidential image" contrasted sharply with that of the politically inexperienced Wendell Willkie who had never been elected

---

[12] Dunn, S., 1940: FDR, Willkie, Lindbergh, Hitler: the Election Amid the Storm, (New Haven: Yale University Press) 2013. p. 189.

to any public office. Only when the Republicans accused FDR of being a "warmonger" did FDR start making campaign speeches. He pointed out that isolationists were hurting the country by opposing any buildup of U.S. Armed Forces. FDR stressed that if this country were forced into war, it would need to be ready.

In hindsight, it is rather amazing that voters gave FDR a third term in the 1940 election. The economy was still in a deep recession and FDR was urging Americans to prepare for a war that they desperately wanted to avoid. Perhaps people began to fear that Hitler's string of successes in Europe and his crippling bombing raids on England might embolden him to come after the militarily weak United States. The reality began to sink in that war might be inevitable. *"Asked how they would vote if there were no war, voters favored Willkie by a 5.5 percent margin, reflecting disillusion with the New Deal and disaffection over the third term issue. But when confronted with the possibility of fighting, they preferred Roosevelt by a far larger percentage..."* [13]

It was clear to President Roosevelt (but not yet to the American people) that this country's best tactic was to help the British survive their onslaught and defeat Germany. This strategy held out the hope that there would be no need to send U.S. troops into battle. FDR issued an executive order *lending* Britain some badly needed destroyers in exchange for long-term *leases* on British bases. This allowed FDR to provide England with military aid without seeking approval from Congress. Although Wendell Willkie stated that he was in agreement with FDR's "lend-lease" proposal *"to extend to the opponents of force the material resources of this nation,"*[14] after the deal was finalized, Willkie criticized the President for bypassing Congress.[15] These days we might call that "flip-flopping."

WENDELL WILKIE AS AN ASSET: Within a short time after FDR won the election, Wendell Willkie and FDR started working together. Willkie became an ambassador for the United States, traveling through Europe (England in particular), to be FDR's roving

---

[13] Kennedy, D., <u>Freedom from Fear</u>, (New York: Oxford University Press) 1999.p.463.
[14] Dunn, S., <u>1940: FDR, Wilkie, Lindbergh, Hitler: the Election Amid the Storm</u>, (New Haven: Yale University Press) 2013. p. 178.
[15] Ibid., p. 184.

ambassador. He returned to the U.S in 1941 to help FDR get his "lend-lease" legislation passed. Congress held hearings at which Joseph Kennedy and Charles Lindbergh spoke against providing any aide to Britain. Having Wendell Willkie as a strong proponent of lend-lease was helpful to balance that testimony. [16]

AT WAR: On December 7, 1941, the Imperial Japanese Navy staged a devastating, surprise attack on the U.S. Naval base at Pearl Harbor, Hawaii. It was a day President Roosevelt said, "will live in infamy,"[17]. The administration was especially surprised because talks with the Japanese were ongoing in Washington, DC at the time. The day after the attack, the U.S. declared war on Japan. Three days later, Germany and Italy declared war on the United States. Isolationism was instantly a thing of the past.

Many people believe that World War II did more to save the economy than any of FDR's New Deal programs. Struggling domestic industries were now converted into humming factories producing military hardware and supplies for their best new customer, the United States Government. Franklin Roosevelt receives high marks from historians for his prosecution of the war. As a former Secretary of the Navy, he knew a great deal about military matters. It was FDR who, with the help of his advisors, appointed Dwight Eisenhower as the Supreme Commander of the Allied invasion of Europe. And it was FDR, together with Winston Churchill, the Prime Minister of Great Britain, who poured over maps and decided where the allies would confront the Nazi war machine. This was no easy matter because, by the time the U.S. entered the war, Germany had swallowed up most of continental Europe, was bombing Great Britain and was winning its fight against Russia.

FAILURE TO HELP EUROPE'S JEWS: For years many people believed that FDR wasn't aware that the lives of Jews in Europe were in peril long before war broke out in Europe. We now know that FDR was aware of the Jews' plight and he refused to help in any way. Any doubt about this was eliminated when CBS's 60 Minutes recently aired an

---

[16] Peters, Charles, Five Days in Philadelphia (New York: Public Affairs) 2005). pp. 191-192.
[17] Roosevelt, F.D., Speech broadcast to the nation on December 8, 1941.

interview with a British citizen named Nicholas Winton who had saved 669 Jewish children in the late 1930's. Many of them were there to share their stories of this unpretentious hero. Mr. Winton (now Sir Winton) said he could have saved so many more Jewish children had the United States agreed to let them into the country. He had personally written a letter to FDR about the children and received a return letter denying his request. Was FDR anti-Semitic? Was this cold indifference? Or could other considerations explain the tragic inaction of a man otherwise known for decisive deeds? An exhibit in the Museum addresses this issue and lets people decide this question for themselves.

JAPANESE-AMERICANS: One of the most regrettable events to occur on U.S. soil during WWII was the treatment of many Japanese-Americans. Those living on the West Coast were rounded up and taken to "relocation centers" far from their homes due to vague rumors that they might be aiding the enemy. They were treated like prisoners of war, often losing homes and jobs as well as their freedom. No one can argue that FDR didn't know about this injustice. He personally issued the Executive Order to carry out that internment.

THE YALTA CONFERENCE: In February 1945, as the war in Europe was reaching an end, FDR went to the Crimean resort city of Yalta on the Black Sea to meet with Prime Minister Churchill and Communist Party General Secretary Joseph Stalin, the leader of the Soviet Union, to discuss plans for post-war Europe.

This was FDR's last conference with these allies and important agreements were made. FDR would not live long enough to learn that Stalin did not keep the promises he made at Yalta.

SOVIET RUSSIA AS AN ALLY: It is difficult to understand why FDR regarded Soviet Russia as an ally of the United States. Joseph Stalin was the absolute dictator of Soviet Russia and was known for his ruthless treatment of Russian citizens, especially peasants and minorities. Although the U.S. didn't have a sophisticated intelligence department, FDR must have known from his interaction with European statesmen that Stalin was responsible for the deaths of millions of his own people. Furthermore, at the start of World War II in August of 1939, Stalin and Hitler made a pact. They agreed that if Germany were to invade Poland from the East, Stalin would invade from the West and Poland would be divided between them. They also agreed that Soviet Russia would get Lithuania, Estonia and Latvia. By signing this pact with Germany, Russia had unilaterally negated a previous agreement the Soviet Union had made with France for defense of that country. Stalin was clearly a man who could not be trusted. Stalin became the sudden and unexpected ally of the U.S. and Great Britain only because Germany broke its nonaggression pact with Stalin and sent three million soldiers to fight Russian troops. Given this history, trusting Stalin to keep the agreements he made at Yalta can only be thought of as terribly naïve.

CHANGING OF THE GUARD: FDR was elected for a fourth term to finish the job of ending the war. His Vice President this time was the former Senator from Missouri, Harry S. Truman. Although Henry Wallace had been FDR's Vice President since 1940 and had been serving in FDR's administration since 1933, he was regarded as an outspoken liberal at a time when the country was becoming more conservative. FDR was seriously ill and, in case his health should become a campaign issue, his advisors wanted him to run with someone whose policies were more middle-of-the-road. Only 82 days after his fourth term began, President Roosevelt died from a massive stroke on the afternoon of April 12th, 1945. Harry Truman was sworn in as the new President that same day. It is surprising – and frankly, rather alarming – to learn that FDR never once briefed his new Vice

President on anything substantive about the war. Nor did he even hint at the Manhattan project in New Mexico, where scientists were racing to develop an atomic bomb that could be used to defeat the Japanese. At our next Museum, we will see how Truman handled his new job.

Visiting FDR's Presidential Museum

4079 Albany Post Road, Hyde Park, New York 12538
Telephone: (845) 486-7770

website: www.fdrlibrary.marist.edu

Museum Hours:
>   9am-5pm, November through March
>   9am-6pm, April through October
>   Closed Thanksgiving, Christmas, and New Year's Day

Admission Fees: (Tickets are sold at the Henry A. Wallace Center.)
$18 for a joint ticket for both the Museum & the Home of FDR. These tickets are valid for 2 days (see below "Things to Do and See in Hyde Park"). Individual tickets for FDR's Home are $10 each.
$9 for an individual ticket to visit only the Presidential Museum
$6 for seniors (62 & older)
Free for children 15 and under

Group Visits: School groups are admitted at no charge. All school groups should coordinate their visit with the Museum's Education Department.

PARKING: Free lot at the museum

Suggestions for Lodging

Bed and Breakfasts

Inn in the Woods
>   32 Howard Boulevard Extension, Hyde Park, NY 12538
>   (845) 229-9331; Website: **www.innthewoods.com**
>   Free Wi-Fi; free Parking; free Breakfast
>   Outdoor whirlpool spa; no pets

Journey Inn Bed and Breakfast
> 1 Sherwood Place, Hyde Park, NY 12538
> (845) 229-8972; Website: **www.journeyinn.com**
> Free Wi-Fi; free Parking; free Breakfast

Le Petit Chateau Inn Bed and Breakfast
> 39 West Dorsey Lane, Hyde Park, NY 12538
> (845) 437-4688; Website: **www.lepetitchateauinn.com**
> Free breakfasts, Free wi-fi, Free Parking;

Hotels

Hampton Inn & Suites Poughkeepsie
> 2361 South Road, Poughkeepsie, NY 12601
> (845) 463-7500; Website: **www.hamptoninn.com**
> Free Wi-Fi; free Parking; free Breakfast; Indoor Pool
> Pets allowed ($50 fee)

Residence Inn – Poughkeepsie
> 2525 South Road, Rt. 9, Poughkeepsie, NY 12601
> (845) 463-4343; Website: **www.poughkeepsieresidenceinn.com**
> Free Wi-Fi; free Parking; free Breakfast
> Indoor pool; pets allowed ($100 fee)

Suggestions for Restaurants

Many visitors come to Hyde Park to dine at one of the four restaurants of the Culinary Institute of America: (The Institute is often referred to as the "CIA", which we assume has no connection with the Intelligence Agency... although these days, one can't be sure!).

The Bocuse Restaurant – French cuisine
American Bounty – American cuisine
Caterina de Medici – Italian cuisine
Apple Pie Bakery Café

All of these restaurants are located at 1946 Campus Drive, Hyde Park, New York 12538, and all have students who are learning to cook

Except for Apple Pie Bakery, these restaurants include a 17% gratuity that is automatically added to the bill and require a reservation for lunch and dinner which can be made by telephone: 845-471-6608 or on the Institute's website: **www.ciachef.edu**

In general, lunch at CIA restaurants is from 11;30am-1pm and dinner from 6pm-8:30pm (and for the Apple Pie Café, 8am-5pm); however, remember the students are doing the cooking, and when they are on a school break, the restaurant will not be open. Also, times vary for different reasons, so please make a reservation for all but the Café if you want to eat at one of these restaurants.

Calico Restaurant and Pastry Shop (American/French) only 7 tables
6384 Mill Street, Rhinebeck, NY 12572
(845) 876-2749; Website: **www.calicorhinebeck.com**
Closed Mon &Tues; Dinner reservations are recommended
Wed-Sat: 11am–2pm; 5:15pm–8pm; Sun: 11am–2:pm

PC's Paddock Restaurant (American)
273 Titusville Road, Poughkeepsie, NY 12603
(845) 454-4930; Website: **www.pcspaddockrestaurant.com**
Tues-Thurs 11:30am – 9pm; Fri: 11:30am – 10pm
Sat: Noon – 10pm; Sun: 8am – 9pm

Four Brothers Pizza Inn & Restaurant (Italian)
3803 Rt. 9G, Rhinebeck, NY 12572
(845) 876-3131; Website: **www.fourbrotherspizzainn.com**
Mon-Sat 11am–10pm; Sun: 11am-9pm

Clancy's Café and Creamery (American)
815 Violet Ave, Hyde Park, NY 12538
(845) 229-9866;Website: **www.clancyscafeandcreamery.com**
Open 7 days a week, 10am-9pm
Home made ice cream and food;

Mizu Sushi (Japanese/Thai)
4246 Albany Post Road (Rt.9), Hyde Park, NY 12538
(845) 229-8688; Website: **www.mizusushiny.com**
In a shopping center but the interior is nice
Mon-Thurs: 11-10; Fri: 11-11; Sat: 12-11; Sun: 12-10
Mon-Sat: closed for a break from 3pm – 4:30pm

Attractions in the Area

Franklin Delano Roosevelt Home ("Springwood):

On same grounds as the Museum: 4097 Albany Post Road This was FDR's home from 1880 until 1945, when he died The furniture, paintings and books are all like they were then The tourist season is May-Oct, so we suggest reserving a tour in advance even if you're not with a big group to avoid a long wait **To reserve: call 877-444-6777, option 1 or reserve online at recreation.gov (click on "find tours")**; groups of 10 or more must have a reservation anytime of the year: The tour cost is $10 (or $18 for a ticket for both the library and Springwood) Children 15 and under are free; Tickets are sold at the Wallace Visitors Center, 9-5; You can also see an introductory film at the Wallace Center; Daily tours at Springwood start at 9:30am and the last tour is at 4pm during May-Oct; During Nov-April, there are fewer tours per day and the house is closed on Thanksgiving Day, Christmas Day and New Year's Day; You should be aware that the house is not well lit, probably to preserve the contents, but it is somewhat difficult to see into some rooms. FYI: walking on the grounds of Springwood, Valkill and even the Vanderbilt estate is free and offers beautiful views. The Hyde Park trail links all three venues and is open daily during daylight hours at no cost. Trail maps are available at **www.nps.gov/index.htm**

Val-Kill Cottage:

54 Valkill Park Road- Route 9 G, Hyde Park, NY 12538, Eleanor Roosevelt's home ~ 2 miles from Springwood. There is a separate home for the First Lady because Springwood was owned and run by her mother-in-law, and Eleanor did not feel comfortable there. There is a 16-minute film, "Close to Home" and then a tour, which lasts around one hour. It is more interesting than the Springwood tour if you get a guide who knows the history. The fee is $10 (children 15 and under free). As with Springwood, during May-Oct, tours run 7 days a week and reservations are made per the instructions under Springwood above. However, unlike Springwood, during Nov-April, tours at Val-Kill are only available in the afternoon and

individuals cannot reserve for tours during those months. In addition, there are no tours on Tuesdays and Wednesdays during Nov-April. (Closed for Thanksgiving, Christmas and New Year's).

Top Cottage:

4097 Albany Post Road, Hyde Park, NY. President Roosevelt built this retreat in 1938 to "escape the mob at Springwood". It was not open when we were there, so we are anxious to return to see it. You can only enter the property by taking a shuttle from the Wallace Visitor Center, and only in the summer, May-October, with tours at 11:10am, 1:10pm and 3:10pm. The cottage is closed from Nov-April. The cost is currently $10.

The Vanderbilt Manson:

119 Vanderbilt Park Road, Hyde Park, NY 12538. Tours start daily at this well maintained 54 room mansion every hour from 10:am until 4pm. The cost is $10 and children 15 and under are free; The information for reserving a tour, holiday closings and seasonal changes is the same as above under Springwood. You should know that the rooms are dimly lit in this mansion, although not as dark as in FDR's Springwood home.

The Historic Town of Rhinebeck

A charming spot only a short distance (12 miles) from Hyde Park; approximately a 20-minute drive from the FDR library (with no traffic); go North on US 9N/Route 9N. There are many historic mansions such as Montgomery Place in the vicinity (see below)

Walkway over the Hudson River (a pedestrian bridge) is a must

The walk across the span is 1.28 miles long; Go to the entrance in the town of Poughkeepsie. For directions, see the website: **www.walkway@parks.ny.gov;** You can also call (845) 834-2867 for more information. At 61 Parker Avenue in Poughkeepsie there is a parking lot for $5; We parked for free at Pulaski Park, on Washington Street. There is a stairway from Washington Street directly to the Bridge. There is a new elevator entrance at 83 North Water Street in Poughkeepsie, 12601; there is no cost to walk on the bridge; it is only closed for inclement weather

Montgomery Place

This is a 380-acre property near Rhinebeck at 25 Gardener Way, Annandale on Hudson, NY. For GPS, use 26 Gardener Way, Red Hook, NY 12571. Since we don't know what direction you are coming from, you will need to check Google maps or MapQuest or get directions from the Website: **www.hudsonvalley.org** (type in Montgomery Place). From the town of Red Hook, you will follow Route 9G and, after a few miles, turn left on Annandale Road, then left onto River Road to the Mansion. This is another place where people can walk the grounds for free (if there are no special events there), so that might be the best thing to do here since the tour is limited to the first floor of the mansion and the interior needs a lot of work. If you get a good tour guide, the $10 fee might be worth taking the 45 min. tour (children under 3 are free). House tours are only May-Oct at 10:30, 12noon, 1:30 and 3:00. The house is shut for the winter months.

Kykuit, Rockefeller Estate:

381 North Broadway, Sleepy Hollow, NY 10591 (914) 631-8200; Website: **www.hudsonvalley.org/historic-sites/Kykuit (Closed Nov – Apr).** You cannot enter the grounds unless you purchase a tour ticket. There are several tours to choose from. The Grand Tour is $40 (it's 3 hours, so we don't recommend it). The Classic tour is two hours and is $25 for Adults Mon-Thu and $28 Fri-Sun. (there are two other tour choices around the same price as the Classic tour). John D. Rockefeller, the founder of the Standard Oil Company, built the house in 1913 and four generations of Rockefeller's lived there. The last was Nelson Rockefeller who was the Governor of New York as well as Vice President under President Ford. The estate has 18th century style furniture and spectacular views of the surroundings. The art collection in the house and garden includes works by Henry More, Pablo Picasso, Alexander Calder and others. To get there, you must take a shuttle bus from the Visitor Center at Phillipsburg Manor at 381 N. Broadway, Sleepy Hollow, NY 10591

HARRY S. TRUMAN

33RD President – 1945-1953

First Lady: Elizabeth (Bess) Wallace Truman

On April 12, 1945, Vice President Harry S. Truman, who was unknown to many Americans, suddenly became the leader of the world's most powerful nation in the midst of a major war.

When Mrs. Roosevelt gave him the news of the President's death, Truman asked what he could do for her. Mrs. Roosevelt famously responded: *"Is there anything we can do for you? You are the one in trouble now."* [18]

Indeed, many Americans felt that *they* were the ones in trouble now. They would be relying on an inexperienced leader in trying times. Although Truman had served in the Senate for more than 10 years, he had little if any foreign policy experience, and there was

---

[18] McCullough, D., Truman, (New York: Simon & Schuster) 1992.. p. 342.

nothing in his background to make people feel that he would be able to lead a nation at war. FDR, who had earned worldwide respect and admiration during his twelve years in office, was to be replaced by a former haberdasher from Independence, Missouri who had no more than a high school education.

EARLY LIFE: Harry Truman was born in Texas and the Truman family moved to Independence, Missouri in 1890 when Harry was six years old. That same year, at a Sunday school class in the First Presbyterian Church on North Pleasant Street, he met Elizabeth ("Bess") Wallace, his wife to be.

After High School, Truman held various jobs in nearby Kansas City, worked on the family farm, and served for two years as an Artillery Officer in World War I. At some point he found time to court his childhood sweetheart, Bess Wallace, who he married in 1919. In order to support his new bride, Truman opened a men's clothing store with his friend Eddie Jacobson. Their haberdashery eventually failed, and Truman took the job that he later said was the only job he had ever actively sought. He became a local county judge.

SENATOR OF KANSAS: In 1934, Tom Pendergast asked Truman to run for the United States Senate. Tom Pendergast was the head of the powerful "Pendergast Machine," which dominated Kansas City politics and provided Harry with the money to enter the election. Truman won a hotly contested campaign. However, he attracted little attention in the Senate until years later. In 1941 he began investigating how government money was being used for the build-up to World War II. What he found was corruption, waste and fraud. Truman became Chairman of the Senate Special Committee to Investigate the National Defense Program or, as it came to be known, the "Truman Committee." This position gave him a high profile in the Senate and his name appeared in some of the nation's newspapers for a while.

VICE PRESIDENT: Truman never asked for, and apparently didn't even want to be FDR's Vice-President. He was put on the Democratic ticket as a "compromise candidate" for the 1944 Vice Presidential spot. President Roosevelt virtually ignored his new Vice President, failing to include Truman in any substantive meetings, even those concerning the war. Truman didn't attend cabinet meetings or get any briefings on major issues.

"PRAY FOR ME NOW." The day after he was sworn in as President, Truman told a group of reporters: *"Boys, if you ever pray... pray for me now. I don't know whether you fellows ever had a load of hay fall on you, but when they told me yesterday what had happened, I felt like the moon, the stars and all the planets had fallen on me."* Truman's unpretentious style was a radical departure from the refined demeanor of the President the country had grown used to in the past twelve years.

STATUS OF THE WAR: In the fateful month of April 1945, as Truman was being sworn into office, the war in Europe was winding down. It finally ended on May 8, 1945, with Germany's unconditional surrender. However, the war with Japan seemed to have no end in sight. The more battles the Japanese lost in Asia and the Pacific, the more ferociously they fought; and they appeared ready to continue fighting until the last citizen of Japan, whether soldier or civilian, had died. The U.S. hoped that Russia would soon send its military to join American troops in Asia. However, by this time relations between the United States and Soviet Russia had begun to sour. Truman arranged to meet Stalin and Churchill on July 17, 1945 in a German town called Potsdam to discuss strategies regarding the war with Japan as well as post-war matters regarding Europe. Truman hoped that a face-to-face meeting might cause the parties to work better together.

UNITED NATIONS: In the meantime, despite the pomp and

circumstance surrounding Roosevelt's funeral, President Truman insisted that the conference dealing with the opening of the United Nations in San Francisco, scheduled to take place just eleven days after Roosevelt's death, should proceed on time. Truman was an ardent supporter of the long-delayed project of establishing an effective international forum. By June, the Charter of the United Nations was signed by all of the delegates; and surprisingly, the Senate ratified it a month later despite the fact that isolationists, who had prevented the League of Nations from being ratified after WWI, were still in the Senate. In fact, the United States was the first country to ratify the U.N. Charter.

SECRET PROJECT: Until a month after he was sworn in as President, Truman knew nothing about a secret program in New Mexico's desert called the "Manhattan Project" to make an atomic bomb. Although the bomb had not yet been tested and it was not even clear that it would work, Truman promptly set up a committee to consider where and when the bomb should be used, assuming of course that the project was successful.

AGREEMENTS BETWEEN THE ALLIES: Although two months before Roosevelt's death he had made important agreements with Churchill and Stalin during their conference at Yalta, Truman knew nothing about these agreements or even where to locate them. Truman studied everything he could find about that conference and was determined to abide by all of its agreements, including the withdrawal of U.S troops as stipulated at Yalta. Winston Churchill advised Truman not to move any American forces in Europe until it was certain that Stalin would honor his commitments. Truman ignored Churchill's advice. He pulled U.S. troops out of Europe as soon as the war with Germany was over, only to find that Stalin kept his soldiers where they were and annexed those areas to the Soviet Union. In direct violation of Stalin's agreement at the Yalta meeting, Poland, Czechoslovakia, and many other countries, including East Germany, were trapped behind what Churchill called an "Iron Curtain."

A FAST LEARNER: Others who were fighting alongside the U.S in World War II had not been invited to participate in any of the FDR/Churchill/Stalin conferences. Among those who very much resented not being present at those meetings was a group of soldiers called "the Free French" led by General Charles de Gaulle. De Gaulle opposed the Vichy government in France that had allowed the Nazis to take control of his country without a fight. Although De Gaulle's soldiers in exile referred to themselves as the provisional French government, FDR and Churchill refused to recognize them as such and, for the most part, ignored any of de Gaulle's suggestions during the war. Now that the war with Germany was over, De Gaulle refused to follow Truman's order to pull back his forces; and further, he sent French troops into Italy, Syria and Lebanon, areas that had been under French control before World War II. Hearing this news, Truman issued an immediate order to stop all shipments of guns and other equipment to France. That instantly solved the problem.[19] For a President with no previous foreign policy experience, his decisive performance was remarkable. Fortunately, Harry Truman had a sharp mind and learned his new job quickly. He relied on common sense and spoke the truth as he saw it, and he expected his team to do the same. Truman certainly made mistakes along the way. He once signed an order that he had not read. It cut off Lend-lease to our allies, and turned out to have serious repercussions.[20] However, he swiftly learned from his mistakes and always took responsibility. He placed a famous sign on his desk, which said, "THE BUCK STOPS HERE."

AT THE POTSDAM CONFERENCE: Nine weeks after the end of the war in Europe, Joseph Stalin and Winston Churchill met with President Truman at Potsdam. While there, Churchill lost his reelection as Prime Minister and Clement Attlee, the new Prime Minister of Great Britain, quickly took Churchill's place at the bargaining table. Now that Churchill and FDR had been replaced by the "newbies," Attlee and Truman, Joseph Stalin became more intransigent than ever regarding Eastern Europe. This may explain why Potsdam was not as productive as President Truman had hoped. However, Stalin did confirm that Russian troops would join the allies to fight against the Japanese. Stalin actually brought the subject up at the beginning of the conference, as if he were eager to join the war against Japan. Truman wanted Russian troops to fight the Japanese in Manchuria while the U.S would fight

---

[19] Truman, M., Harry S. Truman, (New York: William Morrow & Co.,) 1972. p. 247.
[20] McCullough, D., Truman, (New York: Simon & Schuster) 1992.. p. 382.

them in Japan. Truman was unaware that the Japanese had removed most of their forces from Manchuria because they were needed elsewhere.[21]

While at Potsdam, Truman received a message letting him know that the test of the atomic bomb had been successful and he decided then and there to tell Stalin that the U.S had a powerful, new kind of weapon. The Museum tells us something that Truman didn't know. The atomic bomb was not news to Stalin. His spies had already told him about it. In fact, one of them was working at the Manhattan Project in New Mexico. Stalin kept mum about this for obvious reasons: He didn't want to disclose that he had spies in New Mexico, and he realized that now he could rely on the atomic bombs to gain the Soviet Union new territory in the far East without his troops having to do much fighting, a reason perhaps for Stalin's eagerness to join in the war against Japan.

WAR IN THE PACIFIC: By the summer of 1945, the war in the Pacific had been raging for three and a half years. The issue was no longer whether the allies would defeat Japan. Even the Japanese military had concluded that they would probably lose the war within a year.[22] The problem was how to get the Japanese Emperor to agree to an unconditional surrender. Despite devastating "fire-bombing" that incinerated large parts of nearly all of its major industrial cities, Japan continued to fight on. It was estimated that a ground invasion of Japan would cost between 250,000 and 500,000 American lives, as well as the lives of countless Japanese civilians.[23] And yet, that invasion seemed inevitable barring some unexpected change. That surprise came on August 6th when an American atomic bomb utterly destroyed the city of Hiroshima. Truman promised more such devastation if Japan did not immediately surrender. For three days the world was stunned by Japan's silence. On August 9th a second bomb was dropped on Nagasaki. That same day, Russian troops arrived in Manchuria to enter the war against Japan. Incredibly, despite the imminent threat of more unimaginable carnage, Japan began to haggle over details about the

[21] Morison, S, The Oxford History of the American People, (New York: Oxford Univerity Press) 1965. p. 1047.

[22] McCullough, D., Truman, (New York: Simon & Schuster) 1992.. p. 437.

[23] Dallek, R., Harry S. Truman, (N.Y.: Times Books, Henry Holt & Co, LLC,) 2008. p. 26.

future role of the Emperor. After five more days, the long awaited announcement of Japan's surrender finally came on August 14th.

As Stalin had predicted, he was able to reap territorial rewards after only a few days of fighting: He gained control over what is now called "outer Manchuria". In addition, Korea was split into two sections. North Korea was made a Communist zone to satisfy Stalin, and South Korea was declared a democratic zone to satisfy the U.S. and Great Britain. All of the countries that were absorbed by Soviet Russia after World War II were ruled by a Communist regime. They took their orders from Stalin, who had absolute power. There was little or no free enterprise, no market economy, and definitely no freedom of speech. As Stalin's troops annexed Poland, Czechoslovakia and other Eastern countries close to Soviet Russia, a new conflict between nations, one that threatened all mankind, began. It was called, the Cold War.

POSTWAR AMERICA: World War II was followed by a remarkable period of peace and prosperity. But this was not a smooth transition. American soldiers came home to shortages in jobs and housing, rising prices and labor strikes. Labor strikes had especially angered the public when they interrupted major industries, and their anger turned toward the President. Truman's polling numbers dropped to 32% due to his apparent inability to either prevent or quickly settle these disruptive disputes. Republicans benefited and took control of both houses of Congress in the 1946-midterm elections. Congress reacted to the labor disruptions by passing the Labor Management Relations Act of 1947, better known as the Taft-Hartley Act, which put limits on the power of labor unions, including their ability to strike. Truman vetoed the legislation but Congress overrode the veto, and the Taft-Hartley Act became law.

POSTWAR EUROPE: In early 1947, the economies of Greece and Turkey were failing. The British announced that they could no longer afford to send those countries economic and military aid and hoped the United States would assume that responsibility. The fear was that if Greece and Turkey went bankrupt, they would fall under Communist control. Truman wanted to adopt a foreign policy position that was so far-reaching that he felt he had to ask Congress to approve it. In a hard-hitting speech before both Houses of Congress, Truman made his case and received bi-partisan support to give military and economic aid, not only to Greece and Turkey, but also to any country that might later need help in trying to fight off the spread of Communism. The cost was staggering. For Greece and Turkey alone, it would amount to hundreds of millions of dollars (equal to billions in today's dollars). Using economic aid to stop the spread of Communism became known as the Truman Doctrine, and might be considered this country's first major offensive in the Cold War.

Europe was in terrible shape, not only from war related damage, but also due to the extraordinarily severe winter of 1946-47. Large areas suffered from heavy floods, others endured drought, and the entire continent experienced widespread starvation and unrest. Truman's response to this colossal need was the Marshall Plan, an expensive program that the Truman administration proposed and fought for in 1948. In urging Congress to go along, Truman argued that Communism takes hold in economically deprived areas. He pointed to the rise of the Communist Parties in France and Italy. The $5.3 billion price for the Marshall Plan was colossal for that time, dwarfing the cost of the aid to Greece and Turkey.[24] Reluctant members of Congress flew to Europe to see if the conditions warranted so much money from the United States. Congress finally agreed to adopt the Marshall Plan only after the Communists took over control of Czechoslovakia in February 1948.

1948 ELECTION: In 1948 Truman faced his first Presidential election. It should have been an easy win for New York's Governor

---

[24] Morison, S, The Oxford History of the American People, (New York: Oxford Univerity Press) 1965. p. 1057.

Thomas E. Dewey, the Republican candidate. Not only was Truman's popularity at an all time low, he had also lost the support of the solidly Democratic South by advocating for civil rights reform and by ordering the integration of the Armed Forces. Truman's Executive Order No. 9981, which is displayed at the Truman Museum, states that it is "*the policy of the President that there shall be equality of treatment and opportunity for all persons in the armed services without regard to race, color, religion or national origin.*" There was strong resistance in the military to this order, and it was not fully implemented for many years.

Truman ran a vigorous, "whistle-stop" campaign, crisscrossing the country giving speeches from the rear platform of his train denouncing the "do-nothing" Republican Congress and earning the applause of audiences who shouted, "Give 'em hell, Harry!" Truman's blunt style contrasted sharply with the uninspiring speeches of Dewey, who didn't seem to work very hard at campaigning and must have thought he had the election in the bag.

Newspapers and pollsters forecast Dewey's win. Before the votes were counted, the Chicago Tribune had already distributed papers with the boldly printed headline: "Dewey Defeats Truman." It turned out that people loved it when Truman gave the Republicans hell. He was not only reelected President; his Party also won the majority of both houses of Congress on his coat tails.

RED SCARE: The country was also in the grips of a paranoia that would later be called, "the Red Scare." Joseph McCarthy, a Republican

Senator from Wisconsin, had begun making sensational but unsubstantiated charges of Communist infiltration in the Truman Administration. The Republican Party was still reeling from the surprising upset of the 1948 election, and was quite willing to fan the flames of public fear. By fostering distrust of the government, Republicans also dampened public enthusiasm for new government programs. Most of Truman's proposed "Fair Deal" legislation failed to materialize.

Truman and Israel

RECOGNITION OF ISRAEL: In 1948 Truman was also faced with the question of whether the United States would recognize the new State of Israel, which declared its independence after the British pulled out of Palestine.

Background: In 70 AD Roman Legions finally breached the walls of Jerusalem, destroyed the Temple that was the center of Jewish life, dispersed the Jewish people and renamed the land of Israel, "Palestinia." A small number of Jews remained in the new province of Palestinia (later called Palestine), ruled by Rome and living among Arabs, Greeks, Turks and Romans. For two millennia, Christians, Muslims, Jews and Druze lived side by side. Jews in the diaspora often found refuge in Palestine, particularly during the Spanish Inquisition in the 15th and 16th centuries and during the Pogroms of Eastern Europe in the 19th and 20th centuries. During the 1850s, Jews began purchasing inhospitable land from the Turks who ruled the Ottoman Empire, draining swamps, irrigating sand dunes and establishing farms and settlements between the Mediterranean Sea and the Jordan River. With the disintegration of the Ottoman Empire at the end of the First World

War, the British took control of Palestine and Iraq as "protected mandates," and agreed to set aside a coastal strip of Palestine as a Jewish homeland. The rest of Palestine was named "Transjordan," and was turned over to a Hashemite King from the Arabian Peninsula. That became the independent nation of Jordan and was admitted as a member of the United Nations in 1946. The coastal strip of Palestine was to remain a British mandate until the scheduled removal of British troops, on May 14th, 1948. Displaced European Jews who had survived the massacres of World War II were now seeking refuge in Palestine as their ancestors had been doing for centuries. The difference was their numbers. Now they came by the thousands. 1947 saw violent Arab protests on the remaining strip of Palestine, not only between Arabs and Jews, but against British installations as well. In an effort to quell the violence, the British proposed a partition that would further divide the coastal strip into Jewish and Arabic sections. The "partition proposal" was accepted by some of the Arabs and all of the Jews in the mandate.

Truman's Dilemma: Truman's trusted friend and Secretary of State, George C. Marshall, rejected the notion of an independent State of Israel and favored transferring the British mandate to the United Nations until all of the Arabs would agree to a partition plan. Since Arabs throughout the Middle East were threatening war if the Jews set up any State at all in Palestine, Marshall's idea seemed unrealistic to say the least. But Marshall was concerned that the flow of oil to Western countries would cease if war broke out. Pressure to recognize Israel was strong, including from most State governors and many in Congress. Mrs. Roosevelt tendered her resignation as U.S delegate to the United Nations when she thought Truman was going to decline to recognize Israel. In the end, on May 15, 1948, precisely at the official end of the British mandate, Truman recognized Israel on behalf of the United States. As soon as the new nation declared its independence, the threatened Arab attacks began and the U.S. declared its neutrality. Truman refused to ship military equipment to the Israelis as forces from Jordan, Egypt, Syria and Iraq invaded.

BERLIN AIRLIFT: After the war, Germany was divided into West Germany and East Germany. West Germany was rebuilt mainly with money from the United States with the intent that it would become an independent, democratic country. East Germany was a Communist country controlled by Stalin's troops. Even though Berlin was located deep within Communist East Germany, it was divided into four separate zones: The U.S., France and Great Britain each had a zone that together were called West Berlin; and Soviet Russia had the fourth zone, called East Berlin.

In 1948, the Soviets cut off supplies to West Berlin from West Germany that kept the more than 2 million West Berliners alive. Stalin blocked access by land and sea and threatened to starve the population of West Berlin into submission. In response Truman ordered an airlift of supplies to West Berlin that Truman's advisors were certain would fail. It required 600 planes a day, 24 hours a day and seven days a week to supply enough food and coal to keep the West Berliners alive. A year later, Stalin finally backed down and ended his land and sea blockade.

THE KOREAN WAR: In September 1949 the Soviet Union successfully tested its own atomic bomb. In the ten months that followed, China's government fell to the Communists and the Soviet-sponsored government of North Korea invaded South Korea and swept through most of that country. Truman feared that Japan and Southeast Asia would be the next to fall. With United Nations backing, he sent American troops to retake and defend South Korea. It turned out to be a long war, battling for one muddy hill after another. Truman wanted to reestablish the border between North and South Korea at the 38th parallel, which was agreed to in 1945 at the end of World War II.

However, General Douglas MacArthur (who in 1933 had disobeyed Hoover's orders and forcefully evicted protesting Veterans from their makeshift camp near the Capitol in Washington, D.C.) exceeded his authority once more. Ignoring a personal directive from President Truman, MacArthur issued a public statement advocating advancing troops into North Korea and into China if necessary to gain a full surrender of North Korea rather than agreeing to an armistice at the 38th parallel. He followed this up with a similar letter to Congress, ending with the statement: "There is no substitute for victory."[25] Truman believed such a move would escalate a limited war into a global conflict, pitting U.N. forces against the combined military might of China and the nuclear-armed Soviet Union. MacArthur's actions in defiance of the Commander in Chief left Truman no choice but to dismiss the General. However, MacArthur remained extremely popular with the President's critics who liked the General's more hawkish anti-Communist stance.[26] After more than two years, the war in Korea was grinding to a stalemate, troop morale was low, and Americans at home were growing war-weary. Truman decided not to run for reelection. He had served for almost two terms and, like our first President, he thought that was long enough for one person to hold that powerful position.

NATO: Many Americans felt that they could not allow other countries to fall to Communism because of the fear that the Soviets would try to make the U.S. a Communist country as well. This was one of the principal reasons that Truman created the North American Treaty Organization (NATO). Truman wanted to prevent Soviet expansion **and to** have a strong alliance with European democracies to lessen the chance that war would break out again in that part of the world. The members pledged to come to the aid of any NATO country that came under attack. This was a rather astounding commitment for the United States, a country that for most of its history had followed George Washington's advice to avoid international entanglements and take advantage of its isolated position in the world. However, aircraft carriers and long-range bombers had shattered the notion that vast oceans could protect us. The world was beginning to shrink and was

---

[25] Dallek, R., Harry S. Truman, p. 118.
[26] Morison, S, The Oxford History of the American People, (New York: Oxford Univerity Press) 1965. p.1071.

growing increasingly interdependent. Today NATO consists of 28 countries that we are pledged to defend. (See **www.nato.int** for a list of members.)

TRUMAN'S FAIR DEAL: Truman thought that in his second term he was going to be able to advance his "Fair Deal," which included legislation for civil rights as well as for national health insurance, aid to education, improvements in the unemployment system, increased aid to farmers and benefits for Veterans. Despite having a Democratic controlled Congress, most of these reforms failed to get through Congress. Nearly two decades later, when President Johnson signed his landmark Medicare Law, he visited the Truman Museum and handed the first Medicare cards, numbered 1 and 2, to Harry and Bess Truman, recognizing that it was his old friend Harry Truman who had begun the fight for that historic legislation with his proposal of the "Fair Deal in 1948."

1952 ELECTIONS: As the 1952 conventions drew near, the widely popular General Eisenhower agreed to be the Republican nominee for President. During his bitter campaign against the Democratic candidate, Adlai Stevenson, Eisenhower took aim at Truman's handling of the Korean War. In fact, he criticized the very policies that he had encouraged Truman to follow. Now, as a Republican candidate, he was promising to go to Korea and end what he now called, "Truman's war." President Truman was furious.

TRUMAN'S LEGACY: Domestically, some would claim that Truman did not achieve much; others would say that he paved the way for later advances in civil rights and federal assistance for the sick, the elderly and the unemployed. Abroad, he stood by our European allies with the Truman Doctrine, the Marshall Plan, the Berlin airlift and the establishment of NATO. He demonstrated that he could hold the line on Communist expansion in Korea. Above all he was able to keep Germany and Japan, our former bitter enemies, as important allies.

POST PRESIDENCY: After leaving office, Truman continued to do what he loved best: reading history and corresponding with colleagues and friends. Initially Truman received no pension or compensation after leaving office and he turned down lucrative business offers for fear of commercializing the office of the Presidency. However, he was a good lobbyist. He was able to convince Congress to pass a law in 1958 providing for a pension of $25,000 per year for former Presidents. [27] Today Presidents continue to get their presidential salaries for life.

Truman's relationship with Dwight Eisenhower, whose Museum we will visit next, grew estranged, and the rift between these two never healed.

---

[27] McCullough, D., Truman, (New York: Simon & Schuster) 1992. pp. 963-964.

Visiting Harry Truman's Presidential Museum

500 West U.S Highway 24, Independence, MO 64050

GPS users: Use Independence Avenue if Highway 24 doesn't work

Telephone: (816) 268-8200; Toll Free: (800) 833-1225

Website: **www.trumanlibrary.org**

Museum Hours:
> Mon-Sat: 9am-5pm; Sunday: 12 noon-5pm
> Closed Thanksgiving Day, Christmas Day and New Year's Day

Admission Fees:
> $8.00   Adults
> $7.00   Seniors (Ages 65 & older)
> $3.00   Children (Ages 6-15)
> Free   Children (Ages 5 & under)
> There is no admission fee to enter the Museum Store

Touring the Museum/Photography:
> The Museum is designed for self-guided activities.
> Visitors may take pictures in the Museum *without flash*

Special Rates for Groups of 15 or More
> In order to get a group rate, you must pre-book a reservation before you come. To do this, contact the Museum by either calling (816) 268-8221 or by email to **Truman.library@nara.gov**. **For groups, the per person discounted rates are: Adults: $5.75, Youth $3 and School $2.**

Guided Tours:
> For no extra cost the "15 person or more" groups can have a guided tour; however, <u>the group must give the Museum at least four weeks advance notice in order to get a tour guide</u>.. See

above under "Special Rates for Groups" for contact information.

Parking:

Parking is free for Museum visitors

Suggestions for Lodging

Drury Inn & Suites (*8.6 miles from Museum.*

Mailing address: 20300 East 42nd South, Independence, MO 64057
(816) 795-9393; **Website: www.druryhotels.com**
Physical address: Exit 17 from Interstate 70
4215 South Little Blue Parkway
Free Wi-Fi, free parking,
Free breakfast, free hot food and drinks at 5:30 each night
Indoor swimming pool; pets allowed, $10 per night;
Rooms in the front are quieter (away from highway).

Holiday Inn Express & Suites Independence (*9.2 miles from Museum*)
19901 E. Valley View Parkway, Independence, MO 64057
816-795-8889; **Website: www.ihg.com**
Free Wi-Fi, free breakfast, free parking, indoor salt-water pool;
Pets allowed, $25 for entire visit

Staybridge Suites Kansas City-Independence (*7.4 miles from Museum*)
19400 East 39th Place South, Independence, MO 64057
816-994-2700; **Website**: **www.staybridgesuites.com**
Free Wi-Fi, free breakfast, free parking
Outdoor salt-water swimming pool Memorial Day – October 27
Pets allowed, $75 per week, $150 for more than one week

Comfort Suites Independence (*8.7 miles from Museum*)
19751 E. Valley View Parkway, Independence, MO 64057
(816) 373-9880; **Website: www.comfortsuites.com/mo191**
Free Wi-Fi, free breakfast, free parking, indoor salt-water pool
Pets allowed, $25 per night

Higher Ground Hotel (*1.1 miles from Museum*)
200 North Delaware Street, Independence, MO 64050
(816) 836-0292
Free Wi-Fi, free breakfast, free parking, no pets, no smoking
Website: **www.highergroundhotel.com**
Closest to the Truman Museum and on the same street as the

home where the Trumans lived (219 North Delaware Street).

Suggestions for Restaurants

City Market

    20 East 5th Street, Kansas City, MO, 64106

    (816) 842-1271

    Website: **www.thecitymarket.org**

    Several Restaurants and Grocery/Deli stores with different hours

    Farmers Market is every Sat & Sun, 8am-3pm

FINE DINING: Dinner only

Novel Restaurant (American)

    815 W. 17th Street, Kansas City, MO, 64108

    (816) 221-0785

    Website: **www.novelkc.com**

    Tues-Sat: 5:30pm-10pm; Dinner only

    Best to make reservations; <u>Beware: steep steps to the restaurant</u>

Le Fou Frog (French)

    400 East Fifth Street, Kansas City, MO, 64106

    (816) 474-6060

    Website: **wwwlefoufrog.com**

    Tues-Thurs: 5:30pm–10pm; Fri-Sat: 5pm-11pm: Sun:5pm-9pm

ITALIAN: Lunch & Dinner; great for kids

Salvatore's

    12801 East 40 Highway, Independence, MO, 64055

    (816) 373-2400

    Website: **www.Salvatores.us**

    Mon-Thurs: 11am–9pm; Fri: 11am–10pm; Sat: 4pm–10pm

Square Pizza

    208 W. Maple, Independence, MO, 64050

    (816) 461-2929

    Website: **www.squarepizzasquared.com**

    Sun-Thurs: 11am–9pm; Fri-Sat: 11am–10pm

Bella Napoli Restaurant

    6229 Brookside Blvd, Kansas City, MO 64111

    (816) 444-5041

    Website: **www.kcbellanapoli.com**; go to website for Deli hours

Mon-Thu: 11am–9pm; Fri-Sat: 11am–10pm; closed Sunday
Deli: Mon-Fri: 10am-6pm; Sat: 9am-5pm; Sun: 11am-3pm

Attractions in the Area

Family Home of the First Lady

219 North Delaware Street, Independence, MO 64050. (816) 254-9929, at the southeast corner of Truman Road and Delaware Street. Harry Truman lived here after Bess Wallace's mother became ill. June-October: tours 7 days a week from 9am-4:30pm. NOTE: due to budget cuts, tours may not always be available on Sun & Mon. Nov-May: Closed Mondays (could include more days of closure depending upon availability of funds). Regular closing is all federal holidays. $5 admission fee except that those under age 15 & under are free, but they must have a ticket to be admitted; Obtain tickets at the Park Service Office: 223 Main Street. Tickets are first-come-first-served so get there early because they tend to go quickly (ticket office opens at 8:30am);

Truman's Boyhood Home

909 Waldo Street (the southeast corner of River Blvd & Waldo St.) Truman lived there from 1896 to 1902The house was sold and now visitors can only look at the exterior

The National World War I Museum at Liberty Memorial

100 West 26th Street, Kansas City, MO 64108 (816) 888-8100; Website: **www.theworldwar.org**. This is a great museum with movies and exhibits about World War I. Regular Hours: Tues-Sun: 10am-5pm; closed on Mondays except open on holiday weekends such as Presidents Day. The Museum is closed on Christmas Day, New Year's Eve, New Year's Day and May 31st. Summer Hours:(Memorial Day through Labor Day): Sun-Thurs: 10am-5pm and Fri-Sat: 10am-6pm: 'Over There Café" is open for lunch, 11am-3pm. Tickets are for two consecutive days and include galleries, special exhibits and Liberty Memorial Tower: $14 Adults (active military get 50% off with ID) $12 Seniors (65+) and Students (18+ with ID) $8 Youth (6-17); 5 and under are free. See the website for other discounts and group rates

Starlight Theatre

4600 Starlight Road, Kansas City, MO 64132 (816) 363-7827Website: **www.kcstarlight.com**Broadway shows and concerts: outdoor venue. Closed in winter: Open: April to early October. Box Office: Summer: Mon-Fri: 9am-6pm; Sat: 10am-4pm but box office stays open on performance days. Ticket prices vary (see website for events and pricing);

Zoo in Kansas City, MO

6700 Zoo Drive, Kansas City, MO 64132 (816) 595-1234. Website: **www.kansascityzoo.org. Summer Hours**: Memorial Day-Labor Day: Weekdays: 8am-4pm; Weekends: 8am-5pm; **Winter Hours**: Weekdays: 9:30am-4pm; Weekends: 9:30am-5pm Closed: Thanksgiving, Christmas and New Years Day. Admission: 12 50 for Adults: (12 to 54; $11.50 for Seniors (55+); $9.50; for Children (3 to 11); Two years and under are Free. BEFORE YOU PAY, ASK ABOUT THEIR "PACKAGES"

The Nelson-Atkins Museum of Art

4525 Oak Street, Kansas City, MO 64111 (816) 751-1278. Website: **www.nelson-atkins.org**. Admission is free however parking is currently $8 Open: Wed, Sat & Sun: 10am-5pm: Thurs-Fri: 10am-9pm: Closed: Mondays & Tuesdays, and these holidays: July 4, Thanksgiving, Christmas Eve and Day, and New Years Day. Don't forget to see the sculpture garden. The Rozzelle Court Restaurant is open for lunch and dinner.

For additional places to stay and eat and for things to see and do, go to the website: **www.visitindependence.com**

DWIGHT D. EISENHOWER

34TH President – 1953-1961

First Lady: Mamie Doud Eisenhower

Like George Washington, Dwight David Eisenhower, or "Ike," as he was affectionately called, had been a war hero before he became President of the United States. Therefore, before talking about his Presidency and the important lessons it has taught us, we begin this chapter with the role Ike played in winning the war against Germany and Italy as it is told in the WWII section of the Dwight D. Eisenhower Presidential Museum in Abilene, Kansas (shown below).

WWII BACKGROUND: Just as understanding the Great Depression is important in order to prevent repeating the mistakes made during that crisis, learning about World War II and its aftermath is essential in order to avoid military mistakes in the future. Unfortunately, subsequent Presidents have chosen to engage in military conflicts such as in Vietnam and Iraq, unfortunate confrontations that were costly in terms of both blood and treasure, that produced more harm than benefit to the U.S. and its allies, and that could have been avoided. However, there can be no doubt that World War II directly threatened America and its allies and needed to be fought and won to preserve a democratic way of life.

The Second World War began in 1939 with Germany's "blitzkrieg" invasion of Poland. But some would say it really began 20 years earlier. In 1919 thousands of Germans gathered in their capital city of Berlin to protest the harsh terms of the Treaty of Versailles that ended World War I. The treaty forced Germany to pay huge reparations and to surrender territory to the victorious nations. When the depression hit, Germany's already weak economy was decimated. Along came Adolf Hitler and his Nazi party who blamed Germany's troubles on intellectuals, Communists and minorities, particularly the Jewish population, which they vowed to eliminate. When Hitler became the German Chancellor, he restored German pride, rebuilt the military and lifted the economy. However the German people paid dearly for those gains. Hitler turned Germany into a fascist state, ruling with an iron fist and brutally suppressing any opposition to his nationalistic and racist regime.

As Germany's dictator, Hitler made no secret of his aim to rid his country of minorities and to expand Germany's borders to provide more territory for what he called his "master race of Aryans". It is surprising that, although leaders of Great Britain and France saw Germany's military buildup and heard Hitler's outrageous rants, they did nothing to stop him even as he threatened to invade his neighboring countries. They feared another World War more than they feared this tyrannical new German "Führer." Hitler annexed Austria in 1938 with no opposition. In March of 1939 his troops took control of Sudetenland and later the rest of Czechoslovakia without any pushback from the West. In September of 1939 his army invaded

Poland. This finally caused Great Britain and France to declare war on Germany because they had promised to come to Poland's aid if it were attacked by Germany; however, not much help was forthcoming from either country. With the Soviet Union invading Eastern Poland as per its pact with Germany, the Polish cause was hopeless. Interestingly, Germany claimed that it had to invade Poland to protect German-speaking people who lived there. This sounds familiar. Russia has used a similar pretext for its actions against Ukraine. History definitely repeats itself. Western powers didn't do much to interfere with Russia's invasion.

In 1940, Hitler's troops easily swept through and took control of Belgium, Luxembourg, the Netherlands and France. The Western leaders realized too late that appeasing Hitler had been a mistake. The time had passed when Germany could be easily defeated. It now had built up its military and added resources from the countries it had invaded. The German economy was strong and getting stronger every day. With what seemed to be an invincible Air Force, the Germans began a fierce bombing campaign against Great Britain. Luckily for the rest of the world, Hitler committed one of his greatest mistakes in 1941: he broke his pact with Russia and sent 3 million German soldiers to the East to fight the Soviets, forcing his military to fight a two-front war.

President Roosevelt knew that it would be difficult to avoid war with Germany.   He felt that if Great Britain fell, Hitler's next step probably would be to attack U.S. ships and the United States itself. Great Britain did not have the money needed for the boats, tanks, fuel and ammunition needed to adequately defend their country; so FDR was able to get his "Lend-Lease" plan (discussed in the FDR chapter) passed by Congress in March of 1941. Lend-Lease enabled FDR to ramp up the manufacture of U.S. military equipment; although the U.S. had a long way to go to be war-ready. Although FDR knew that he could not avoid war with Germany, he had been counting on negotiating a peace agreement with Japan so that he could avoid fighting a two-front war. With the sneak attack on Pearl Harbor in December 1941, FDR had no choice but to engage with Japan as well.

IKE ENTERS THE FRAY: At the end of 1941, just days after the United States entered World War II, Ike was assigned to the War Plans Division in the Office of George C. Marshall, the Army's Chief of Staff. Marshall recognized that Ike was an excellent war strategist who was hard working, extremely organized and not afraid to take risks. General Marshall posted Ike to command American troops in London in June of 1942 and, sometime between June and November 1942, FDR decided that Allied troops should begin confronting the enemy somewhere outside of Europe in order to gain experience they would need for a landing in France that would take place in the future. The place selected by FDR and Churchill for this initial thrust was North Africa, which turned out to be just what the inexperienced Allied troops needed – including Ike, who had never been in combat duty in his approximately 25 years in the army. The operation was called "Torch", and Ike was in charge of all Allied forces, not just Americans, that took part. This experience probably gave Ike the confidence he would need later to lead an enormous amphibious landing in France near the end of the war, called "Operation Overlord." By the end of 1943, Ike and his team had successfully conducted landings in Africa and Southern Europe and had learned to work together as a team. In addition, Ike demonstrated his negotiating skills during the Italian surrender of September 1943.

DESCIPHERING GERMAN MESSAGES: One of the most famous items on display in the Eisenhower Museum is the fabled "Enigma Machine," so named because it held the secret code that Germans used to send messages to dreaded U-boat submarines that stalked the Atlantic sinking allied ships.

The capture of the "Enigma" machine allowed the U.S. and its allies to decipher the enemy's messages and thwart their attacks. Although the Germans would constantly change their machines and their codes, the allies were able to keep enough mathematicians and other technology experts at work to overcome those changes. It is said that cracking the codes of the Enigma machines allowed the allies to win the war several years before they would have done so if they had not captured the machine.

OPERATION OVERLORD: In December of 1943, Ike was appointed as Supreme Commander of the Allied invasion of Europe and he was put in charge of Operation Overlord, a top-secret plan for the invasion of France. It would be the largest amphibious invasion in the history of warfare. This surprise attack from England would require a combination of ships, small boats, paratroopers and airplanes from all of the countries allied against Germany. Its mission was to establish a beachhead from which the allies could drive the German army not only out of France but also from every other country Hitler had seized. Ike commanded troops from the United States, Canada, Great Britain, Australia, New Zealand and the other allied forces.

Courtesy of the Library of Congress

The invasion began on June 6, 1944 (now celebrated as "D Day") with landings on the French beaches of Normandy. Operation Overlord turned the tide of World War II and has been immortalized in books and movies. It required years of meticulous and clandestine planning. Even deciding which beaches would be suitable for such a massive assault was a major undertaking. The sandy beaches of Normandy were chosen because the Brittany coast was too far from England, the coastal areas of Holland were flooded, and the currents of Belgium were too strong. As the military hardware began to be secretly assembled on the coast of England, ground troops, naval forces and pilots had to be secretly trained for the mission, which took years of work and deception.

As D-Day approached, the Germans began to detect military activity in England, and they suspected that an invasion was coming soon. To disguise where the landing would take place, Ike's troops dropped mannequins on parachutes far away from the real landing sites and used radar-jamming devices to make the German's believe that a landing was taking place somewhere other than Normandy. One of these mannequins is on display at the Eisenhower Museum (see below).

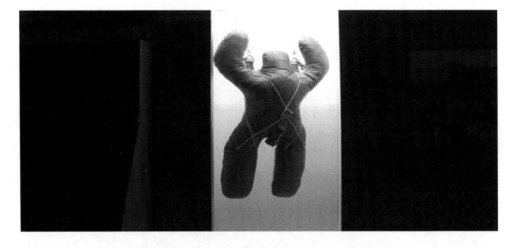

German spies were fed false information to fool the German military. However, on June 5, the day the landing was supposed to take place, a coded message was sent to French resistance groups, instructing them to destroy railroad and telephone lines and do whatever they could to stop the Germans from advancing to the landing sites. And then severe weather in the English Channel forced the invasion to be postponed until the 6th. As it turned out, the Germans were not expecting a landing on either the 5th or the 6th because the weather for both days was unfavorable. In addition, Hitler was certain heavily fortified Normandy would not be the target of the landing, and therefore did not have as many soldiers manning those fortifications as one would have expected. Nevertheless, the allies suffered heavy casualties on June 6th, especially on Omaha Beach. American troops died while still in the water or as they scrambled ashore. The bold landing on June 6, 1944 was only the beginning of Operation Overlord. The troops that survived the dash across the beach and past the enemy positions, and the paratroopers that landed behind enemy lines, had to fight for nearly another year until Germany finally surrendered on May 7, 1945, only days after Adolf Hitler committed suicide. A formal surrender ceremony took place the following day, May 8th. But "D Day," June 6th was selected to be the day celebrated around the world every year.

IKE's POSTWAR POSITIONS: The end of the war was not the end of Ike's illustrious career. Under President Truman, Ike served as the Army Chief of Staff. Truman even urged Eisenhower to run for President as a Democrat in the 1948 election rather than run for reelection himself. Truman made the extraordinary offer of being Ike's Vice-Presidential running mate.[28] However, Eisenhower said he preferred private life and, instead, accepted the position of President of Columbia University. In 1950, at Truman's request, Ike returned to public service. He took a leave of absence from Columbia to become the first commander of the North Atlantic Treaty Organization (NATO) in Europe.

CAMPAIGNING FOR PRESIDENT: Later in 1950, Ike abruptly decided to run for President in 1952 as a Republican. His "I LIKE IKE" campaign buttons were seen everywhere and he won in a landslide after promising that, if elected, he would go to Korea "to stop the war." (See "KOREAN WAR" below). In 1953, Ike became the first Republican to occupy the White House since Herbert Hoover had left it twenty years earlier.

MUTUALLY ASSURED DESTRUCTION: (The "MAD" years); The United States had changed dramatically since the Great Depression. The U.S. was entering the age of television and space exploration; but it was also facing the threat of nuclear war. It seemed

---

[28] McCullough, D., Truman (New York: Simon & Schuster, 1992) p. 584.

that only the threat of a nuclear confrontation would prevent Communism from engulfing freedom-loving people everywhere. The Russians had exploded an atomic bomb long before experts had predicted. The Chinese mainland had fallen into Communist hands under Mao Tse-tung and had threatened South Korea. People were instructed to install shelters in their backyards and basements to protect them from bombs and radioactive fallout.

Basement Fallout Shelter

RED SCARE CONTINUES: Senator Joseph McCarthy continued a ruthless campaign begun during the Truman administration to purge the United States of people in government and in the entertainment industry that he claimed were Communist party sympathizers, or "Reds." Since McCarthy and Eisenhower were both Republicans, the new President had to try to curb McCarthy's activities without dividing his Party. It turned out that television did the job for Ike. After a series of blistering Congressional hearings had featured McCarthy accusing innocent people of being "Reds," the day finally came when McCarthy was the subject of a Congressional investigation himself. People who owned television sets watched the legal proceedings in their living rooms while crowds of others gathered in stores where television sets were on display to watch McCarthy finally being challenged. McCarthy's credibility collapsed when it became clear that he had manufactured the evidence used to make his outrageous accusations.

IKE AS PRESIDENT: Eisenhower was the first President to hold televised press conferences, however these were not live performances. Ike was not good at ad-libbing, so his press secretary, Jim Hagerty, insisted on editing out any mistakes Ike made before the public could see them. After awhile, even this war-hero President was forced to surrender to the demand for instant news ... blunders and all. [29]

KOREAN WAR: By the time Eisenhower took office, the world was polarized as never before. The Soviets had built an "Iron Curtain"[30], separating Eastern Europe (including East Germany) from the West and the Soviets had backed North Korea's invasion of South Korea. When the United States, South Korea and U.N. forces started winning, Chinese Communist troops entered the war on the side of North Korea. The sudden and successful advance of thousands of Chinese troops, who lacked good weapons but who were good at guerrilla warfare, is well documented in Jim Newton's book, *Eisenhower, the White House Years*. [31] Ike fulfilled his campaign promise and went to Korea to seek an end to that war. He concluded that continued conventional combat would lead to a stalemate at best and he therefore threatened the North that he would use nuclear weapons if they did not stop their attacks. This ominous threat got North Korea to agree to an armistice. This meant that there was no peace treaty, but only an agreement that the 38th parallel would remain the demarcation line between the Communists in the North and a democratic state in the South. The 38th parallel still remains a Korean tripwire that threatens future conflict. Many Americans didn't like this result and accused Ike of being soft on Communism, a phrase that was becoming a political weapon in the United States.

---

[29] Shenkman, R., Presidential Press Conferences History News Network, George Mason University, 2001, (online at hnn.us/article/221)
[30] McCullough, D., Truman (NY: Simon & Shuster) 1992. p. 383.
[31] Newton, J., Eisenhower, the White House Years (New York: Doubleday) 2011. pp. 80-84

Ike took a similar stance against Soviet Russia's aggression, relying on the threat of nuclear retaliation rather than conventional warfare. By Ike's second term, the Soviets began to shift their strategy, sometimes using economic assistance rather than weapons and brute force to get countries to partner with Soviet Russia. An example of this is the crisis involving Egypt and the Suez Canal discussed under the subheading of PEACEMAKER in this section of the book.

While Eisenhower greatly reduced the military budget for conventional arms, he significantly expanded U.S. spending on research and development in nuclear and space technology. Eisenhower established the National Aeronautics Space Administration (NASA) but he didn't live to see astronauts walk on the Moon. In a tribute to his foresight, the Museum created an exhibit displaying items from NASA, including a piece of rock brought back from the Moon.

Near the end of Ike's first term, he suffered a heart attack so severe that more than three months after his attack, even though he had begun to work part-time, Ike was not able to give his State of the Union Speech in person. A clerk read it to Congress for him.

THE PEACEMAKER: Despite his precarious health after his heart attack, Ike concluded that, "*the peace of the world was still at stake*" and felt that he was "*called once again to be its peacekeeper.*"[32] Crises were developing in Central Europe and the Middle East. President Eisenhower's view of himself as a peacemaker was corroborated by many local newspapers and had the effect on the public that Ike wanted. According to voter surveys taken in 1956, a majority disliked Ike's domestic policies; however, when he declared shortly before the election that he would not permit the U.S. to become involved in armed conflict either in Central Europe or in the Middle East, Americans voted in a landslide to give Ike a second term as President. After the election several newspapers ran the headline "Victory for Peacemaker."

There were others who were unhappy with Ike's foreign policies. Just before the election, on October 18, 1956, Walter Lippmann wrote a column complaining that Ike's "peace making" was nothing more than giving up without a fight and living with the status quo. As evidence,

---

[32] Newton, J., Eisenhower, the White House Years (New York: Doubleday) 2011.. p. 82.

Lippmann referenced the armistice with Korea and the Suez Canal crisis, in which Ike insisted that Israel, France and England accept the unilateral actions taken by the President of Egypt, Gamal Nasser to nationalize that international waterway.

The Suez Canal Crisis is a good example of the often-inconsistent foreign policies of the Eisenhower Administration. President Nasser had adopted a neutral policy regarding the Soviet Union and the West, and therefore sought financing from both "sides" for a huge dam he wanted to construct. The U.S. and Britain responded with an economic deal, as did the Russians. After Nasser had accepted the U.S./British offer, Ike's Secretary of State, John Foster Dulles, retracted it because: *"Nasser was becoming increasing influential as a leader of neutralist sentiment throughout the world."*[33] Dulles was afraid other countries might emulate that neutral posture rather than side with the United States.[34] For Foster Dulles, being neutral was unacceptable. The U.S. retraction caused Nasser to retaliate by seizing control of the Suez Canal and using the canal's revenue to pay for his dam; this in turn caused Israel, France and Britain to try to reclaim international control of the canal. According to the Museum, Ike demanded that they call off their attack because he was worried that Russia would be drawn into a war with the West over this matter. Nasser emerged as a hero for the cause of Arab and Egyptian nationalism while France and Britain lost most of their influence in the Middle East.[35] Some in Congress and in the press were angry with Ike because they felt he should have supported U.S. allies.

During this same period, the Hungarian people revolted against the Soviet-imposed policies of its government, expecting the United States to come to their aid. President Eisenhower did not. Russian troops rolled into Hungary unopposed and took control of the country. The Museum infers that Ike thought it was more important to keep the peace with Soviet Russia rather than to risk war. President Washington would have agreed with this. The problem is that Radio Free Europe had broadcast appeals to the Hungarian people to resist communist

---

[33] Smith, J., Eisenhower in War and Peace (NY: Random House) 2012. p. 691
[34] Kinzer, S., The Brothers: John Foster Dulles, Allen Dulles and Their Secret World War (NY: Simon & Schuster) 2011. p. 128
[35] Encyclopedia Britannica (www.Britannica.com)

control, leading the Hungarian students who started the revolution to believe that the U.S. would help them become a democratic country.

COVERT OPERATIONS: While Ike was presenting himself as a peacemaker, he was approving covert operations to have the CIA topple foreign governments that were not willing to go along with the United States' agenda. At times this meant replacing a democratic government with a dictator. A report released by the State Department in 1985 defines covert action as *"activities that the CIA might undertake in other countries to accomplish a U.S. foreign policy objective without the hand of the U.S. government becoming known or apparent to the outside world."* Although President Truman had approved covert action to, among other things, use radio broadcasts to cause the populace of a country to reject Communism, President Eisenhower took covert action a giant step further. He approved the toppling of governments, only three of which we will describe here; but there were many others. Learning about these covert actions at the Eisenhower Museum came as a shock.

Operation Ajax ousted the first and only democratically elected Prime Minister of Iran, Mohammad Mossadegh. The British government wanted to get rid of Mossadegh because he had nationalized Iran's oil company. Before Mossadegh had arrived on the scene, the Shah who ruled Iran had made a deal with Britain to share in the operation and ownership of that oil company so that most of Iran's oil went to Britain and its allies. This arrangement made the Shah a rich man but it was of little benefit to the Iranian people. Mossadegh learned that the Shah and the British were scheming to get rid of him, so he took immediate action. He swiftly got rid of the Shah and banned all British citizens from Iran. This is why the British reached out to the U.S. for help. It is difficult to understand why Ike agreed to this unless there had been a deal to give some of that oil to the U.S. Operation Ajax authorized a team from the CIA, led by an agent who happened to be the grandson of FDR, to spread false information about Mossadegh and whip up resentment toward him. The Iranian people believed these false stories and became angry enough to throw their Prime Minister out of office. The Shah of Iran returned after Mossadegh was removed and, until the Iranian revolution of 1979, the Shah brutally oppressed those who opposed his rule. The Shah's ornate desk and portrait are among the gifts to the Eisenhowers on display in the museum.

Ironically, it was Ike who told the world that the United States was behind the coup. Ike was eager to answer his critics who said that he was soft on Communism, so he boasted about the operation to reinstate the Shah in his state of the Union address. He inferred that Mossadegh had Communist leanings even though that was not the case. To this day, the Iranian people and their government resent the United States for toppling their democratically elected government and reinstating a ruthless dictator

A second CIA mission toppled the democratically elected President of Guatemala, Jacobo Arbenz Guzman. Guzman's "crime" was repatriating some land owned (but never used) by the United Fruit Company. This large American corporation had important friends in Washington, D.C. including Secretary of State John Foster Dulles and his brother, Allen Dulles who was the Director of the CIA.[36] Again the stated reason for this intervention was that Guzman was a Communist. However historians who study this period claim that Guzman was neutral and wanted to promote business with both the U.S. and Russia. When the President of Guatemala was finally ousted, the CIA installed a "liberator" whose *"first acts included dissolving the Congress, suspending the constitution, disenfranchising three-quarters of the population by banning illiterates from voting, and decreeing repeal of the land reform law that had enraged United Fruit; ten years of democratic government, the first that*

---

[36] Kinzer, S., The Brothers: John Foster Dulles, Allen Dulles and Their Secret World War (NY: Simon & Schuster) 2011. p. 156.

Guatemalans had ever known, were over."[37]

In 1957, the Dulles brothers felt that the President of Indonesia, Achmed Sukarno, was moving his country toward Communism. There were already groups of Indonesian dissidents openly rebelling against the Sukarno government, so all the CIA had to do was to give the rebels money, weapons and bombing support when they requested it. Ike stated publically that the U.S. was staying neutral with respect to the Indonesian rebellion; however, a short time later, an American pilot was shot down in Indonesia carrying papers that showed he was from the CIA. After that, Ike ordered the CIA to desist. He then provided money and other assistance to the Sukarno government. It leaves one to wonder why the CIA went in to topple the Sukarno government in the first place.

Indeed, it leaves one to wonder whether any of the governments that were toppled during the Eisenhower Presidency were ever a real threat to the U.S. President Eisenhower seems to have been unduly influenced by the Dulles brothers, Secretary of State John Foster Dulles and C.I.A. director Allen Dulles, who had their own reasons for actively seeking out these foreign entanglements. The American people continue to live with the negative consequences.[38]

DOMESTIC AFFAIRS: Nearly a century after the abolition of slavery, African-Americans were still continuing to struggle for their civil rights. As late as 1957, many States continued to claim that segregated schools were "separate but equal." The Supreme Court finally disagreed. Their opinion in <u>Brown v. Board of Education</u> changed the simmering debate over civil rights. It found that segregated schools were unequal and violated fundamental rights granted by the U.S. Constitution. The world watched history unfold on their television screens when, as a result of that landmark Supreme Court decision, nine African-American children attempted to enroll in Little Rock Central High School. Unfortunately the Governor of Arkansas, Orval Faubus, prevented them from entering the school building. After an ugly standoff, Eisenhower ordered federal troops to

[37] Kinzer, S., <u>The Brothers: John Foster Dulles, Allen Dulles and Their Secret World War</u> (NY: Simon & Schuster) 2011 p. 173.
[38] Ibid

escort the children into their classrooms.

Ike is remembered for this forceful action. However, the Museum points out that the President acted only to enforce the law and failed to speak out against segregation as a moral issue. A Museum exhibit about this era states, *"While some black leaders thanked Ike for his actions, many historians consider Eisenhower's lukewarm support of Brown v. Board of Education as one of his major limitations as president."* To Ike's credit, it should be noted that he ordered the District of Columbia and the entire federal government to integrate racially. His order pertained to all federal offices as well as the Military. Although President Truman had already requested that the military be desegregated during his administration, the request was largely ignored. After Ike's order, they finally complied. Ike also proposed and signed the Civil Rights Act of 1957 to protect the voting rights of minorities and called for a Commission on Civil Rights as well as a Civil Rights division to be created in the Justice Department. Unfortunately, Southern Democrats watered down the legislation, and even these laws were difficult to enforce.

An important reminder of the Eisenhower years is an extensive network of Interstate Highways. We were certainly grateful for the speedy and scenic highways that made our more than 8,000-mile road trip to film the museums in this book so enjoyable.

The Museum explains that Eisenhower's main purpose in building the Interstate Highway System was to accommodate the growth of automobile ownership and to facilitate the buildup of the suburbs. In addition, as a military man, Ike wanted to make sure that, in the event of an emergency, troops could move in and people could be evacuated quickly.

U-2 FLIGHTS: By the mid 1950s, the Central Intelligence Agency (CIA) began deploying high altitude U-2 reconnaissance spy planes like the plane depicted in the exhibit below. Along with spy satellites, U-2 planes were keeping the U.S. apprised of Soviet military movements.

Scale model of U-2 spy plane

These specialized aircraft took high-resolution pictures from the stratosphere from an altitude of 70,000 feet showing Soviet missile sites and providing other valuable information. In 1960, the Soviets shot down one of these planes and captured its American pilot, exposing this secret program to the world. Eisenhower denied the existence of these over-flights until he learned that the pilot was still alive and being held in a Soviet prison. The consequences of this unfortunate event cannot be overstated. In the months prior to the notorious "U-2 incident," the relationship between Soviet leader, Nikita Khrushchev, and Eisenhower had showed signs of warming. A summit meeting in Paris had been planned to discuss arms reduction and other issues aimed at reducing Cold War tensions. Immediately before the summit meeting, Eisenhower refused Khrushchev's request to apologize for sending U-2 spy planes into Soviet air space. Khrushchev responded to this rebuff by leaving Paris with his staff before any substantive discussions had begun. Relations between the two superpowers worsened and the Cold War heated up once more. This was particularly true in Berlin, where one year later, the Soviets began constructing the infamous Berlin Wall.

FAREWELL WARNINGS: In his farewell address to the nation at the end of his second term, Eisenhower warned of the potential danger posed by the new, "military industrial complex." He urged Americans to guard against *the potential for the disastrous rise of misplaced power.* He may have been referring to the increasing influence of the defense industry or, perhaps, to a dangerous tendency to rely on sophisticated armaments and military means as a first resort to any crisis. Many members of that "military industrial complex" had urged him to launch a nuclear attack against China during the Korean War; however, President Eisenhower refused to do so. Eisenhower had used the threat of nuclear war as a bluff that he was never called upon to use. Whether he would have done so, and under what circumstances, remains a matter of speculation. In his historic, farewell speech, Eisenhower cautioned: " *Only an alert and knowledgeable citizenry can compel the proper meshing of the huge industrial and military machinery of defense with our peaceful methods and goals, so that security and liberty may prosper together.*" [39]

President Eisenhower and his Administration steered this country through eight years of the Cold War without bringing it to the brink of nuclear war. The same cannot be said for John F. Kennedy, whose Presidential Museum we will visit next.

---

[39] Eisenhower, D., Farewell Radio and Television Address to the American People, January 17, 1961 (www.presidency.ucsb.edu by Gerhard Peters and John T. Woolley, the American Presidency Project.)

Visiting Ike's Presidential Museum and Boyhood Home

200 S.E. 4th Street, Abilene, KS 67410

(785) 263-6700 or (877) 746-4453

Website: www.Eisenhower.archives.gov

Museum Hours:
Regular Hours: Aug-May: Mon-Sun: 9am-4:45pm
Summer Hours: June & July: Mon-Sun: 8am-5:45pm
Closed Thanksgiving Day, Christmas Day and New Year's Day

Museum Admission Fees (includes admission to all buildings
including Ike's boyhood home)
$10   Adult (16-61)
$9   Senior (62+)
$2   Child (6-15)
Free: Ages 5 & Under and Active Military with valid ID

Tickets are sold in the Visitors Center where there is a 25-minute orientation film.

The Museum recommends that when you leave the Visitors Center you go to the Boyhood Home. The entrance door is on the south side. A tour guide provides information on the history of the Home.

From the Boyhood Home, it is suggested that you go to the Museum located to the east of the Home. The Museum suggests that you take approximately two hours to cover the 35,000 square feet of exhibits covering the life of the 34th President.

After you have toured the Museum, you might want to go to the Place of Meditation that is the final resting place of Dwight D. Eisenhower, his wife Mamie, and their first-born son, Doud Dwight

Tours:

Except for the Boyhood Home, there are no guided tours, however, the exhibits are self-explanatory.

Adult Groups:

Adult groups of 20 or more are eligible for a reduced admission rate (currently $9 per person) if they have made reservations in advance with the museum. For reservations ask for Visitor Services when you call the Museum (785-263-6700). Groups without reservations are welcome, but they don't get the special reduced rate. The Museum asks that all members of a large group wear some type of badge so that they may be easily identified at the Museum admission desk. <u>One payment in cash, check or credit card for the entire group is requested.</u> For small groups, admission may be paid individually at the Museum

School Groups:

Students visiting with an "organized school group" are admitted free of charge. One adult for every five students is also admitted for free. All other adults with the group must pay the regular fee. An "organized school group" is a group of students who are in grades K through 12 and whose attendance on the field trip is associated directly with a recognized school (public, private or home). For questions about eligibility and to register in advance, please call Visitor Services at the Museum.

Parking

Parking is free for Museum visitors.

Accessibility

All areas of the Museum are handy-cap accessible.

Suggestions for Lodging

Note: When a train comes through Abilene at night, chances are you're going to hear it. This seems to be true of all nearby towns, so you might want to bring earplugs.

Abilene's Victorian Inn & Gift Shop (Bed & Breakfast)
   820 NW Third Street, Abilene, KS 67410
   (785) 263-7774 or (888) 807-7774
   Website: **www.abilenesvictorianinn.com**
   Free breakfast, free parking & free Wi-Fi
   Children 6yrs old and above are welcome

Four Seasons RV Acres
   2502 Mink Road, Abilene, KS 67410
   (785) 598-2221; Website: **www.4seasons.com**
   Pets allowed; Outdoor swimming pool; store on premises
   Sales/service and parts for RVs on premises

Holiday Inn Express
   110 E. Lafayette Ave, Abilene, KS 67410
   (785) 263-4049
   Website: **www.hiexpress.com/abileneks**
   Indoor swimming pool, free breakfast & free parking
   Free Wi-Fi; Pets allowed ($20 fee); five smoking rooms

Suggestions for Restaurants

BREAKFAST and/or LUNCH ONLY:

The Dish:
   207 North Cedar Street, Abilene, KS 67410)
   (785 263-3836
   Mon-Fri: 11am-2pm
   TAKES ONLY CASH;
   Lunch only: healthy foods

Amanda's Bakery & Bistro
   302 N. Broadway, Abilene, KS 67410
   (785) 200-6622
   Tues–Fri 8am–4pm; Sat: 9am-3pm; Closed Mondays
   Fresh baked goods and fresh vegetables
   They have antiques & collectables in the store for sale

Hitching Post
>100 SE 5th Street, Abilene, KS 67410
>(785) 263-1868
>Open 7 days a week
> 6:00am – 2:00pm; Serves Breakfast and lunch
>American home style cooking; Free parking;

GRILLS:

Ike's Place:
>100 North West 14th Street, Abilene, KS 67410
>(785) 200-6278
>Sun-Thurs: 11am-10pm; Fri-Sat: 11am-2am
>free parking; free Wi-Fi; smoking on the patio
>Burgers but also has vegetarian options

Joe Snuffy's Old Fashioned Grill
>209 W First Street, Abilene, KS 67410
> (785) 263-7802
>Mon, Wed, Thu: 7:am – 8:30pm; closed Tuesdays
>Fri: 7am – 9pm; Sat: 6am – 9:30pm;
>Sun: 6am – 8:30pm: Okay to smoke on the patio

M & R Grill
>1720 N Buckeye, Abilene, KS 67410
> (785) 263-9819
>Website: **www.mandrgrill.com**
>Tues-Sat: 11am – 10pm; Sun: 11am – 3pm; Closed Mondays
>Burgers/salads, sandwiches; free parking;

PIZZA:

Tossed n Sauced
>306 NW 3rd Street, Abilene, KS 67410
> (785) 263-2121
>Sun-Thurs: 11am – 9pm; Fri-Sat: 11am-10pm
>free Wi-fi

Attractions in Abilene, Kansas

The Great Plains Theatre   **(live shows and movies)**

> Unfortunately the Theatre burned down but plans to reopen in another building. If your are interested, call or check their website before your visit.
>
> (785) 263-4574: Website: **www.greatplainstheatre.com**

Dickson County Heritage Center

> 412 South Campbell Street, Abilene, KS 67410
>
> (785) 263-2681, Website: **www.heritagecenterdk.com**

(This is the site of Three Attractions:)

> **The Historical Museum**, depicting life on the plains before Kansas Statehood;
>
> **The Museum of Independent Telephony**, and
>
> **The Outdoor Museum**, which features a fully restored and operational 1901 Carousel
>
> $6.00 per adult,
>
> $5.00 for Seniors 62 and over
>
> $2.00 for child 2 – 14 (includes one carousel ride for a child)
>
> Additional Carousel Rides, $2.00 for adults and seniors.
>
> Regular hours: Mon – Fri: 9 – 3; Sat: 10 – 5; Sun: 1pm – 5pm
>
> Summer: Mon – Fri: 9 – 4; Sat: 10 – 8; Sun: 1pm – 5pm

JOHN F. KENNEDY

35th President   1961 -1963

First Lady: Jacqueline Bouvier Kennedy

Driving up to the JFK Museum and Library on the Boston Waterfront is a bit like seeing John F. Kennedy for the first time. After passing a number of unremarkable buildings, one of them suddenly grabs your attention. The Museum presents a bold, fresh face to the world, evoking memories of the inspiring young President whose powerful story it preserves.

The building sits on a ten-acre site that has been landscaped with shrubs and trees native to Cape Cod, a place that President Kennedy loved. Inside the Museum you will be guided by films, recordings and television broadcasts of President Kennedy. His voice and images will transport you back to the 1960s.

When "JFK" or "Jack" Kennedy (he seldom used the name John) took his oath of office in January 1961, color television sets were still a rarity and the event was telecast in black and white. Many of the nation's communities and public accommodations were similarly limited to – and sharply divided along those color lines as well. The civil rights movement was taking its tumultuous first steps, while the

Cold War teetered toward catastrophe.

On your walk through President Kennedy's Museum you will see how the youngest President this country has ever elected would deal with its increasingly violent racial division; how he would strive to reduce world tensions; bring the world back from the brink of nuclear destruction; energize the U.S. to put a man on the Moon and lead the nation to the "New Frontier" of outer space. He would do all of this while suffering from several serious health problems, including excruciating back pain, Addison's disease and intestinal disorders.

EARLY YEARS: Jack was born in 1917 to a large and prominent Catholic family, which, despite its wealth, struggled against the prevalent anti-Catholic sentiment of Boston society. His father, who would later serve as FDR's U.S. Ambassador to Great Britain, was a successful banker and real estate mogul who had married the mayor's daughter, Rose Fitzgerald. Boston's large Irish population had helped to elect John "Honey Fitz" Fitzgerald as the first Catholic mayor of that city.

Jack is in the white shirt at the top left of this family photo, taken at the Kennedy compound in Hyannis port on Cape Cod.

His older brother, Joe Jr., may have snapped the picture. Jack and

Joe were fiercely competitive in school, sports and every aspect of their lives. Joe had set his sights on a life in politics, but when Joe was killed in World War II, Jack stepped up and took his place. At the museum, you can see the young man as he attended fine schools and traveled through pre-war Europe. You will hear JFK tell you in his own words, the suspenseful story of the sinking of PT Boat 109, which he commanded as a Navy Lieutenant in World War II. The story of his heroism became a legend.

When asked how he had become a hero, JFK replied,
"It was involuntary. They sank my boat."

But there was much more to the story. On the night that a Japanese destroyer rammed and sank his patrol boat, Kennedy led the wounded survivors on a nighttime swim of several miles, to a remote Pacific island in enemy territory. Kennedy had been on the Harvard swim team and dragged a wounded crewmember through the water by a belt clenched in his teeth. After several difficult days and a number of harrowing incidents, two native islanders paddled up in a canoe. Kennedy gave them a coconut on which he carved a message, giving his position and asking for help, hoping they might find someone who could read it. The story obviously had a happy ending. When the coconut was returned to him, Kennedy preserved it as a desk ornament to remind him of his good fortune.

Coconut with carved message

As those natives paddled away, the young Lieutenant must have wondered whether his carved coconut would be lost, or worse, fall into enemy hands and give away their position. Today it is displayed in a Museum dedicated to his Presidency.

Given the option of returning home to care for his chronically painful back, JFK chose instead to take command of another gunboat and stay in the fight. He would later be awarded the Navy and Marine Corps Medal and a Purple Heart.

With the war over and his brother Joe killed in the Pacific, Jack decided to enter politics. News accounts of his heroism propelled his career. Kennedy's narrative takes us through his terms as a U.S. Representative, a Senator from Massachusetts and his marriage to Jacqueline Bouvier ("Jackie"). The film ends with his nomination by the Democratic Party to run for President in 1960. Running against him was Richard Nixon, a veteran campaigner who was then the Vice President of the U.S. Kennedy chose Lyndon Johnson, the Senate majority leader and savvy Southern politician as his running mate. Kennedy felt that he would need Texas in order to win the election, and he was counting on the fact that Johnson was from Texas to give him that win.

From the theater, visitors enter a replica of a White House corridor with exhibits highlighting important issues in that campaign, including the relationship of Church and State that was then on the minds of many in a predominantly Protestant nation. Some feared that a Catholic President would owe too much loyalty to the Pope and not enough to our Constitution.

On April 21, 1960, in a speech to the American Society of Newspaper Editors in Washington, D.C., candidate Kennedy said: *"Are we going to admit to the world that a Jew can be elected Mayor of Dublin, a Protestant can be chosen Foreign Minister of France, a Moslem can serve in the Israeli parliament – but a Catholic cannot be President of the United States? ... Are we to admit to the world – worse still, are we going to admit to ourselves – that one-third of our population is forever barred from the White House?"* [40]

Another popular exhibit is a replica of the television studio in which the Nixon-Kennedy debates of 1960 took place. These were the first televised Presidential debates, and close-ups of the two men provided valuable lessons for future candidates. Because Nixon had refused make up, his face seemed pale and his beard stubble and perspiration were plain to see. For many viewers, this had a profound effect. Nixon seemed tired and haggard while Kennedy appeared tan, vigorous and youthful.

THE KENNEDY PRESIDENCY: Kennedy won the election by the

---

[40] Kennedy, J., The Religion Issue in American Politics, (www.jfklibrary.org)

slimmest of margins. In his inaugural address, he challenged the nation with his famous demand: *"... ask not what your country can do for you. Ask what you can do for your country."* As if to emphasize his theme that *"the torch has been passed to a new generation of Americans,"* Kennedy spoke on that cold January day with no overcoat, while those listening were bundled up in winter clothes. This vigorous and eloquent young leader was the first U.S. President born in the 20th century, and he stood in sharp contrast to the gray-haired men who had preceded him.

The Kennedys' elegant style was refreshing and the first family was embraced as welcome royalty. The brief period that they occupied the White House has often described as the nation's time in "Camelot." Film stars, poets, artists and writers were frequent visitors to the White House. In the photo below President Kennedy is seen chatting with novelist Pearl S. Buck as Lady Bird Johnson looks on, while Jackie converses with poet Robert Frost.

Soirée at the White House

Women everywhere emulated Jackie's elegant flair for fashion. Jack's good humor and quick wit endeared him to the press and the public as no President in recent memory had done. Although Eisenhower's press conferences were the first to be televised, the public saw nearly humorless films that had been edited. Kennedy, on the other hand, was the first President to do live telecasts of his press conferences in which the public saw a confident President exchanging remarks with the press that were often laced with clever quips and witty retorts.

Beyond the glittering White House, the new President faced a grim reality. Communism was on the march during Eisenhower's term and had reached Cuba, only 90 miles away. Fidel Castro had staged a military coup 1959 and by 1961 Cuba was a one-party, Communist State, dependent on the Soviet Union for military and economic support. In order to strengthen U.S. ties with the rest of its neighbors to the South, Kennedy proposed a ten-year Latin American "Alliance for Progress." And then he learned of a secret plan regarding Cuba, a plot that was brewing before he became President.

THE BAY OF PIGS: Before leaving office, President Eisenhower had developed a secret military mission to overthrow Fidel Castro. It was to be another of his covert operations to be carried out under the direction of the CIA's director, Allen Dulles.

CIA director, Allen Dulles

The CIA had been secretly providing military training and supplies to a group of Cuban exiles in Guatemala and planned to transport them to Cuba where they would instigate a popular revolution against Castro and install a democratic government. President Eisenhower probably assumed that Richard Nixon, his Vice President, would easily defeat JFK and would implement this secret plan.

The CIA strongly advised President Kennedy to go through with the invasion, but they did not tell him that some in the military doubted it could succeed.[41] Moreover, the historian Robert Dallek tells us that neither the CIA nor the Joint Chiefs informed Kennedy that the success of the mission would depend upon considerable U.S. air power aimed at Castro's army.[42] They assumed that the new President would be forced into calling for U.S. air support to save the mission when it began to fail, even though Kennedy had made it clear that he did not want the U.S. to be seen meddling in another country's internal affairs. If the U.S. was implicated, it would ruin the already strained relations the U.S. had with Latin America and it would wreck Kennedy's Alliance for Progress program.[43] Dallek tells us that Kennedy decided

[41] Thomas, E., Ike's Bluff: President Eisenhower's Secret Battle to Save the World (New York: Little, Brown & Company) 2012. pp. 406-407
[42] Dallek, R., Camelot's Court, Inside the Kennedy White House, (New York: HarperCollins) 2013. p. 135

to proceed only because the plan was developed by the astute military mind of Dwight Eisenhower, and he shared the fear that Castro would foment Communist uprisings elsewhere in Latin America if left unchecked. In addition JFK knew that if he were to call off the invasion, his political enemies, as well as the Cuban exiles who were ready to put their lives on the line, would publicly criticize him as being "soft on Communism" a charge that was political poison during the Cold War. [44]

On April 17, 1961, the CIA launched the Cuban invasion, however they had made some fatally flawed revisions. The original plan had called for the Cuban exiles to disappear into the mountains if the anticipated uprising by the Cuban people did not materialize. However, because Kennedy wanted to hide the role of the U.S., the invasion site was moved to the Bay of Pigs, located on the South coast of Cuba, facing away from the United States. Unfortunately, this bay had no nearby mountains into which the exiles could hide. It was surrounded by miles of impenetrable swampland and there was no way for them to escape Castro's forces that were ready and waiting.[45] When news reached Kennedy that the invasion was going badly, he ordered additional air support, but it was not enough to make a difference. Almost the entire invasion force was either captured or killed. U.S. weaponry and supplies were found in abundance and there could be no doubt that the United States was involved.[46]

A despondent President Kennedy went to former President Eisenhower to seek advice. Ike counseled that, rather than getting advice from one person or agency at a time, the proper way to reach a decision is to have all key advisors in one room debating the pros and cons of a prospective mission and to weigh all of their arguments.[47] Ike also told him *There is only one thing to do when you get into this kind of thing: make sure it succeeds;*[48] In other words, winning is more

---

43 Ibid. p. 133

44 Dallek, R., Camelot's Court, Inside the Kennedy White House, (New York: HarperCollins) 2013. p. 137-138

45 Dallek, R., Camelot's Court, Inside the Kennedy White House, (New York: HarperCollins) 2013., p. 135

46 Ibid. p. 144

47 Thomas, E., Ike's Bluff: President Eisenhower's Secret Battle to Save the World (New York: Little, Brown & Company) 2012., p. 406

important than trying to hide U.S. involvement.

President Kennedy took sole responsibility for the Bay of Pigs calamity in a nationally televised address, which may have bolstered his sagging popularity, but the episode greatly affected the mood of the President as well as the beginning of his Presidency. The good news is that he learned a valuable lesson about how to work with his advisors that proved critical during the Cuban Missile crisis, discussed below.

PREPARING TO CONFRONT KHRUSHCHEV: On Kennedy's watch, world tensions had been increasing rather than diminishing. The Soviet Union continued to support Communist uprisings around the world and was tightening its grip on Eastern Europe, East Germany and East Berlin. The arms race and space race now seemed to be tipping in the Soviet's favor. On April 12th 1961 Khrushchev boasted that the Soviet cosmonaut, Yuri Gagarin, had become the first human to travel into space, as well as the first to orbit the Earth. During those depressing days, President Kennedy wanted to engage his protagonist in a personal dialogue with the hope of reducing tensions between them. He arranged for a face-to-face meeting with Soviet Premier Nikita Khrushchev to take place in Vienna in June 1961. In the meantime, he was preparing a bold agenda to present to a special joint-session of Congress on May 25th.

THE FREEDOM RIDERS: His plans were interrupted in early May 1961, when an interracial group of "Freedom Riders" took their seats on buses bound from Washington D.C. to New Orleans. The U.S. Supreme Court had upheld legislation requiring the desegregation of interstate busses, and black Freedom Riders were going to test the law's implementation in the segregated South. They chose seats in the front of the bus as well as next to their white compatriots. A few miles outside of Anniston, Alabama, a Greyhound Bus carrying some of the Freedom Riders was ambushed, emptied and burned by the Ku Klux Klan. A Trailways Bus carrying Freedom Riders was also attacked in Anniston. When those Freedom Riders were pulled from their bus, they were badly beaten by an angry mob, and the local police refused to intervene.[49] Television images of the burned out bus and bloodied

---

[48] Ibid. p. 407
[49] Gadney, R., Kennedy, (N.Y.: Holt, Rinehart and Winston) 1983. p. 107.

faces of the Freedom Riders shocked the entire world.

President Kennedy was reluctant to send federal troops to the scene. His agenda for the country's future depended on support from the ardently segregationist Southern Democrats in Congress. Moreover, he was concerned that prolonged attention to these protests would overshadow the global issues he was preparing to discuss with Khrushchev in Vienna. He feared that worldwide press coverage of racial confrontations in the U.S. would become an embarrassing propaganda tool in the Cold War. Winning that war was uppermost in the President's mind. Therefore, Kennedy's response was coldly pragmatic and politically driven. He merely called leaders of the civil rights movement and told them to call off their protests.[50] However, JFK was forced to take action when local police in Montgomery, Alabama actively joined in a vicious assault on the Freedom Riders. The brawl in Montgomery became a full-blown riot and, three days before his scheduled speech to Congress, Kennedy finally called on federal troops to quell the violence. In order not to antagonize Southern Democrats in Congress, JFK limited his response to a call for law and order rather than a full-throated denunciation of segregation. Kennedy saw this civil unrest as an unwelcome distraction from his main focus: the Cold War and his upcoming meeting with Premier Khrushchev.

TRYING TO "RESET" HIS PRESIDENCY: On May 25th Kennedy addressed a special, joint session of Congress as a prelude to his Vienna Summit meeting. He put forward a plan to meet the Soviet challenge with one military objective and three non-military measures.

Kennedy's military objective was to build up the nation's conventional military strength. If there were to be a confrontation over West Berlin, the Congress would need to provide additional military funding. But, he argued, the hearts and minds of the developing world would not be won over by military might. A different strategy would be necessary to prevent countries in Asia, Africa and South America from aligning with the Communist block. Kennedy offered three, non-military proposals to win the Cold War:

---

[50] Gadney, R., Kennedy, (N.Y.: Holt, Rinehart and Winston) 1983p. 108.

First, he proposed increasing foreign aid to win the allegiance of struggling people by helping them fight hunger and disease. Second, he surprised the nation with a bold new idea: the establishment of a Peace Corps. Thousands of qualified volunteers would travel to underdeveloped countries, learn their local languages and live in the same circumstances as the indigenous people. With no pay except for travel and living expenses, they would work with natives of their host countries, applying their knowledge and skills to implement practical solutions to the third world's most pressing problems.

The final proposal was the most dramatic and far-reaching. It was the ambitious goal of sending an American safely to the Moon and back to Earth before the end of the decade. Despite the enormous costs involved, Congress swiftly approved JFKs entire ambitious program. The concept of landing a man on the Moon captured the imagination of the country and rekindled its pioneer spirit. It also launched a technological revolution that changed the world. The burgeoning Space Age was also the incubator of the ensuing Age of the Computer.

"I believe this nation should commit itself to achieving the goal,
before this decade is out, of landing a man on the Moon
and returning him safely to Earth." (May 25, 1961)

TO FRANCE AND THEN VIENNA: JFK was now eager to meet with Khrushchev and personally engage him in meaningful dialogue. The President was confident that the summit meeting in Vienna would foster a better working relationship. On the way to Vienna, the President and First Lady stopped in Paris to meet Charles de Gaulle.

Jacqueline spoke fluent French and stole the show with her beauty and charm. President Kennedy remarked that he would be remembered as *"the man who accompanied Jacqueline Kennedy to Paris."* Like many Americans, we were glued to our TV set, watching the wonderful reception the Kennedys received in France.

The Kennedys with French Culture Minister André Malraux

While in Paris, Kennedy met with former U.S. Ambassador to the Soviet Union, Averell Harriman, who gave him the following advice: *"Ignore Khrushchev's abrasive words and tone, … don't let him rattle you."* [51] Unfortunately, Kennedy ignored that advice and got into heated arguments with Khrushchev, perhaps failing to realize that much of Khrushchev's bluster was for domestic consumption back in Russia. There also was another reason. The President typically took a large number of medications for back pain, Addison's disease, colitis and excessive weight loss. However, at this time he was experiencing excruciating back pain and was given extra large doses of painkillers, sleeping pills and amphetamines from a doctor who was often referred to as Kennedy's "Doctor Feelgood." These excessive doses may have

[51] Dallek, R., An Unfinished Life: John F. Kennedy, 1917 – 1963, (N.Y.: Thorndike) 2003. p. 402.

impaired his ability to engage properly with Khrushchev. [52]

Khrushchev and Kennedy at Vienna, June 3. 1961

We know from exhibits at the Museum (as well as from Khrushchev's son, who now lives in the U.S. and has appeared in discussions sponsored by the Kennedy Museum) that the Vienna Summit meeting left the Russians feeling that Kennedy was an intelligent but weak President. Before the meeting was over, a bellicose Khrushchev threatened to close off West Berlin, blocking all Allied supply routes to that beleaguered city.

THREATS AGAINST WEST BERLIN: Kennedy returned from Vienna empty handed and disappointed. In the weeks that followed, the threats that Khrushchev had made at Vienna began to materialize. There was now growing concern that Khrushchev was willing to risk war in order to take control of West Berlin. On July 25th, Kennedy addressed the nation to prepare for that possibility. West Berlin, he said, was *"an isle of freedom in a Communist sea;"* and he sternly warned: *"any Soviet attack on West Berlin would be equivalent to an attack on NATO."* It was a televised speech to the nation but the closing words were clearly aimed at Nikita Khrushchev: *"We seek peace – but we will not surrender."*

---

[52] Ibid, p. 471.

People on both sides of the Iron Curtain feared the worst. Nuclear war was no longer a theoretical threat; it was now a present danger. On August 13, 1961, The Soviet Union added to those fears by cordoning off East Berlin, first with barbed wire and then with a tall concrete barrier to prevent East Berlin's citizens and those from other Soviet block countries from escaping to the West. Paradoxically, this had the immediate effect of actually reducing tensions between East and West because fewer refugees were gaining worldwide attention by successfully fleeing to West Berlin. However, Khrushchev may have had a different plan to get the United States out of West Berlin, a plan that would involve arming our neighbor Cuba with nuclear weapons.

CUBAN MISSILE CRISIS: For 13 days in the fall of 1962, the world came to the brink. A riveting exhibit hall in the Museum takes us through the terrifying events of October 1962. It is not hyperbole to say that, during those suspenseful days, mankind faced an imminent threat of nuclear annihilation. The Museum displays once classified memos, including letters exchanged between Kennedy and Khrushchev at the climax of the Cuban Missile Crisis. You can listen to the President's television addresses to the nation and hear recordings of his meetings with advisors, including his younger brother Bobby, his Attorney General. It is chilling to see how the fate of the world depended on the behavior of three very different men – the zealous revolutionary, Cuban Prime Minister Fidel Castro; - the youthful U.S. President John F. Kennedy; - and the shrewd survivor of Stalin's purges, Soviet Premier Nikita Khrushchev.

Films, recordings and exhibits at the Museum show the following events as they occurred:

On Tuesday, October 16, 1962 the President was shown photographs taken from a U-2 spy plane over Cuba disclosing new Soviet medium range ballistic missile installations. These nuclear weapons had been secretly installed in Cuba. The clandestine build up was still progressing rapidly under the guidance and control of the Soviet military with the full approval and cooperation of Fidel Castro.

Kennedy called a team of top military and foreign affairs advisors to the White House and met with them daily throughout the crisis. Listening to recordings of these meetings at the Museum makes you feel as though you are in the room with them. It also makes you realize that "expert" advice can be fatally flawed.

These advisors did not yet know if the Cuban missiles were operational. You can see and hear them guessing on this point. They were certain only of one thing: If (or when) the missiles were fired, they could devastate a large portion of the United States. They considered two options: either a Naval blockade to prevent additional military supplies from reaching the Island, or an air strike on the Cuban missile bases. Neither option would be certain to prevent the launch of a nuclear missile aimed at the United States.

Despite the risk of retaliation, most of Kennedy's advisors advocated an immediate airstrike, hoping to eliminate the Cuban threat. They argued that limiting the U.S. response to intercepting ships at sea could risk a shooting war that could trigger the release of nuclear-armed missiles from Cuba. JFK was against rushing into war and he wanted time to figure out how both sides could avoid it. He tried to understand why Khrushchev would risk a nuclear conflict that no one could win. Only a month before, Kennedy had specifically warned the Soviets that bringing offensive weapons to Cuba would have "grave consequences." Could this threat be related to Berlin? According to documents at the JFK Museum: *"Throughout the crisis, President Kennedy was convinced the missiles in Cuba were linked to the U.S. presence in West Berlin … He feared that if the U.S. were to strike the missile sites in Cuba, the Soviets might respond by attacking West Berlin, a city he had vowed to protect."*

One of Kennedy's big problems was that the Bay of Pigs debacle and JFK's poor performance at the Vienna Summit had left Khrushchev and many others feeling he was weak. Once, when a journalist wanted to write a book about Kennedy's first term, Kennedy asked, *"Why would anyone want to write a book about an administration that has nothing to show for itself but a string of disasters?"*[53] Historian Robert Dallek tells us that when JFK was told about the missiles in Cuba he had just finished reading a news article in which former President Eisenhower was quoted as saying that Kennedy is *"a weak president."* [54]

It is surprising that someone so widely regarded as weak would

[53] Kempe, F., Berlin 1961, (N.Y.: G.P. Putnam's Sons) 2011. p. 486.
[54] Dallek, R., Camelot's Court, Inside the Kennedy White House, (New York: HarperCollins) 2013. p. 295.

have the courage to stand up to his top military leaders and foreign affairs advisors and reject their call for immediate military action. Of President Kennedy's memorable qualities, perhaps the most notable was his ability to keep a clear and level head in a crisis. Rather than respond reflexively, he took the time necessary to act from reason rather than from fear. In the meantime, the public knew nothing of this frightening development. The President wanted time to formulate a plan that might cause the Soviets to stand down. He did not feel he could do that if people heard about the missiles and started to panic. For the first few days, the President continued to follow his normal schedule even to the point of keeping a previously arranged out-of-town engagement.

On Thursday October 18th (the third day of the crisis), the Soviet Foreign Minister, Andrei Gromyko, asked to see the President in the Oval Office. Kennedy wondered if Gromyko would have something to say about the secret developments in Cuba. The answer was no. Either Gromyko himself was in the dark, or he was playing dumb. In the remarkably relaxed and cordial scene pictured below, Kennedy gave no hint of knowing of the Cuban missiles. However, he reminded Gromyko (seated at the center of the sofa) of his prior warnings that offensive Soviet weapons in Cuba would lead to *"the gravest consequences."*

JFK meeting with Andrei Gromyko in the Oval Office

The following day, <u>Friday October 19th</u>, (Day 4 of the crisis) Kennedy left on a previously planned political trip, but returned on Saturday, feigning a cold so as not to arouse suspicion. Much of his time was spent questioning and listening to his advisors.

At the Museum, you can hear Kennedy discussing plans for a Naval blockade. Air Force Chief of Staff Curtis Lemay protested: *"I think that a blockade and political talk would be considered by a lot of our friends and neutrals as being a pretty weak response to this. And I'm sure a lot of our own citizens would feel that it was too."* U.S. Army Chief of Staff Earl Wheeler concurred with the Air Force Chief: *"From a military point of view, I feel that the lowest risk course of action is the full gamut of military action by us. That's it sir."*

Secretary of Defense, Robert McNamara quickly reminded them that it would take considerable time to assemble the large force required for the full gamut of military action, and that a ground invasion would need to be preceded by several days of airstrikes. Curtis Lemay reiterated, *"I don't see any other solution except direct military intervention right now."* J. William Fulbright, the Chairman of the Senate Foreign Relations Committee added: *"I think a blockade is the worst of the alternatives. If you confront a Russian ship – you are confronting*

Russia – and you will have fired the first shot."

Saturday October 20th, (the 5th day of the crisis), Kennedy came to a decision. After further discussion with his White House advisors, the President ordered plans to be drawn up for the plan that none of them had advocated: a Naval blockade of Cuba; and he immediately began working on a speech he would give to the nation. The address would be his first response to Nikita Khrushchev. There was then no "hot line" to Moscow; the two leaders could communicate privately only by sending secure written messages through their embassy offices, a process that could take as much as twelve hours each way. The White House scheduled the President's televised address to be given 48 hours later, stating only that it would be about *"a matter of national urgency."*

The next day, Sunday October 21st, (Day 6), the President was advised that some of the Cuban missiles were already armed with nuclear weapons and that an air strike would definitely not have guaranteed the destruction of all of them. Had he followed the advice of his "experts," Washington D.C. could have been obliterated by then.

On Monday, October 22nd (Day 7) President Kennedy was ready to tell the world about the crisis. Before making that 7 p.m. announcement, he had done several things. He called prior Presidents, Hoover, Truman and Eisenhower as well as the British Prime Minister to brief them on the situation. He received the endorsement of the Western Hemisphere neighbors, (The Organization of American States, of which the U.S. was a member) for his plan to blockade Cuba. He asked a committee of the National Security Council (NSC) to meet daily to oversee planning of the blockade. He provided the Soviet Ambassador a copy of his speech and – most importantly – he sent a two-page message directly to Nikita Khrushchev. This letter, which is available to read at the Museum, says in part: *"... I have not assumed that you or any other sane man would in this nuclear age, deliberately plunge the world into war which it is crystal clear no country could win and which could only result in catastrophic consequences to the whole world, including the aggressor."* At 7 p.m. a stunned audience watched the President announce that the Soviets had placed nuclear missiles in Cuba that could reach anywhere within a radius of 1,000 miles. They would be able to destroy Washington D.C or any city in the South Eastern United

States. He called upon Chairman Khrushchev to *"halt and eliminate this clandestine, reckless and provocative threat to world peace."*

JFK signing Proclamation 3504
Authorizing Naval Blockade of Cuba
Oval Office, October 23, 1962

On <u>Tuesday October 23rd</u> (Day 8), President Kennedy signed Proclamation 3504, authorizing the naval quarantine of Cuba. The U.S. Navy was ordered to establish a blockade, to stop and board any vessel passing within 500 miles of the island and turn back any ship carrying offensive weapons. Naval vessels took their positions and Kennedy sent Khrushchev a message including this passage: *"I am concerned that we both show prudence and do nothing to allow events to make the situation more difficult to control than it already is. With this in mind I hope you will issue instructions to your ships bound for Cuba not to challenge the quarantine legally established by the Organization of American States this afternoon."* Soviet freighters that were bound for Cuba stopped dead in the water before reaching the blockade.

Between October 23rd and October 28th, it seemed that the world literally held its breath. Any mistake could lead to the incineration of cities across the globe and a nuclear winter that no humans might survive. To make matters worse, on October 27th, a U.S. spy plane accidentally strayed into Russian air space near Alaska and was chased out by Soviet MIG fighters, but they were unable to catch the U.S. plane. The U.S. had dozens of fully armed B-52 bombers circling the perimeter of the Soviet Union, refueling in mid-air when necessary. Each plane had nuclear bombs and a set of specific targets; and each one was waiting for orders to unleash its weapons. Luckily, no one jumped the gun,

Khrushchev responded to Kennedy's television statement with a rambling letter. He remained obstinate; claiming that Cuba had demanded better protection after the invasion of the Bay of Pigs. He also insisted these nuclear ballistic missiles were "purely defensive."

On <u>Wednesday the 24th</u> (Day 9), Kennedy received word that most of the previously stalled Soviet ships had turned around and started back toward their homeports. However, two were now continuing toward the blockade. In addition, progress continued at the Cuban missile sites. Workers were still assembling and arming the missiles.

The White House staff wondered if Khrushchev was in control of these events. Why was he pulling back some ships while others were pushing ahead? And why were Cuban missiles continuing to be armed? Perhaps Khrushchev felt that he had enough missiles in place for an effective first strike. We learned at the Museum that each missile was 70 times more powerful than the bombs used during World War II. The Russians also had thousands of troops in Cuba to perform whatever tasks were required to finish their work on the missiles.

On <u>Thursday the 25th</u> (Day 10), at an emergency meeting of the United Nations Security Council, Adlai Stevenson challenged Soviet Ambassador Zorin to admit that his country had secretly installed nuclear missiles in Cuba. When the Ambassador declined to answer, Stevenson presented the Security Council with damning photographs showing the missile installations.

Photos of nuclear missiles in Cuba
U. N. Security Council, October 25th, 1962.

On <u>Friday, October 26 th</u> (Day 11), Khrushchev sent a long and encouraging letter to the White House. He offered to dismantle and remove the missiles in return for a pledge that the U.S. would never invade Cuba. Kennedy and his advisors did not see this letter until early in the morning on Saturday, October 27th.

<u>Saturday October 27th</u> (Day 12) became known as "Black Saturday." Two Soviet ships were approaching the blockade where the U.S. Navy would intercept them. These ships were escorted by Soviet submarines, which added a new level of danger that was not appreciated at the time. The Museum documents that these submarines were armed with nuclear tipped torpedoes. Unaware of this added element of danger, when the ships reached the blockade on October 27th, the U.S. Navy began dropping depth charges to force them to surface. The Museum tells the chilling story of the events at sea on October 27th: Captain V.P. Orlov, a radio officer on Soviet submarine B-59 that day, wrote: *"It felt like sitting in a metal barrel with someone hitting it with a sledge hammer ... We thought – that 's it – the end. ... Savitsky [the submarine commander] became furious. ... He summoned the officer who was assigned to the nuclear torpedo, and ordered him to assemble it to battle*

readiness." Fortunately for all of us, Savitsky's submarine finally surfaced without firing the torpedo that could have triggered a nuclear confrontation at sea; and Captain Orlov lived to tell the tale.

At the White House, the NSC team was still busy figuring out how to respond to Khrushchev's letter when a second letter arrived. This letter sounded as though someone other than Khrushchev had written it, and Kennedy worried that Khrushchev was losing control to more hawkish Kremlin officials. This second letter made a new demand: Before the Soviets would consider any movement of the Cuban missiles, the United States would have to remove missiles it had stationed in Turkey. Actually, Kennedy had previously raised that possibility with his advisors. They spurned the idea as unwise then, and they continued to object to it now. The committee felt that Turkey would object, causing a dangerous delay, allowing more missiles to be assembled and armed in Cuba.

Instead the White House committee recommended ignoring Khrushchev's second letter with the new demand concerning the Turkish missiles. Acting as though they had not received the second letter, they would accept the offer in Khrushchev's first letter, which asked only for a U.S. non-invasion pledge with respect to Cuba. That plan fell apart when they learned the stunning news that radio Moscow had already broadcast the following news: *"Premier Khrushchev told President Kennedy yesterday he would withdraw offensive weapons from Cuba if the United States withdrew its rockets from Turkey."*

On the afternoon of "Black" Saturday, a U-2 spy plane over Cuba swooped low to get close-up photographs and was shot down by a Soviet Surface to Air missile (SAM). The pilot was killed. The mood in the White House became even grimmer. Kennedy had publicly promised immediate retaliation if anyone fired on a reconnaissance plane. He was now given unanimous advice to respond with an immediate attack on the SAM bases. Kennedy's advisors felt that time was running out. They worried that the Soviets were getting ready to make the first strike in an unprecedented nuclear confrontation, and they claimed that this was the moment for military action. Kennedy rejected this advice. He felt that the proposal in Khrushchev's second message was reasonable. The missiles in Turkey were certainly not worth a nuclear war. He wanted to see whether the offer regarding Turkey was genuine. That evening, without informing anyone else, JFK sent his brother Bobby to secretly deliver a proposal to Russian Ambassador Dobrynin, the only one who could wire a message directly to the Kremlin.

The President used this back channel to make the following offer to Khrushchev: The U.S. would publicly pledge not to invade Cuba. The U.S. would also (but without publicly pledging to do so) remove its missiles from Turkey. JFK promised to do this after a period of time had passed. Kennedy's advisors had gone to sleep that night almost certain that the next day would mark the beginning of a war with unknowable and probably cataclysmic consequences. Instead, they awoke to the stunning news that the crisis had ended peacefully.

On the morning of Sunday, October 28, 1962 (Day 13), Kennedy received the response he had been hoping for. Khrushchev had announced on Moscow radio that he had come to an agreement with President Kennedy: Khrushchev would remove the Cuban missiles and Kennedy had pledged not to invade Cuba. Khrushchev made no mention of Kennedy's secret promise to remove U.S. missiles from Turkey. Khrushchev sent a formal letter to Kennedy accepting the terms of the secret proposal that Robert Kennedy had delivered to Ambassador Dobrynin. The letter was signed: *"Respectfully yours, N. Khrushchev."*

After thirteen days of unprecedented peril there was worldwide rejoicing. Khrushchev had discovered that young President Kennedy was truly a man to be reckoned with. Cuban missiles were dismantled and removed under United Nations supervision. Months later, with little fan-fare and not much notice, U.S. missiles were removed from Turkey. As far as we know, Khrushchev kept his promise and never uttered a word about the secret trade. He let the world believe he had simply backed down with nothing more than a promise from JFK that the United States would not invade Cuba.

LESSONS LEARNED: President Kennedy learned an important lesson from the Bay of Pigs: Expert advice is not always correct advice. This time, the President had gathered his experts together to debate their positions, and then he did what he was elected to do. He charted a course for the best possible outcome. Using his good judgment, he reached a successful, honorable and peaceful solution. It is not unreasonable to wonder what the outcome might have been if anyone other than JFK had been the President in October 1962.

Khrushchev may also have learned an important lesson from this crisis: Kennedy was deadly serious about defending West Berlin. According to Frederick Kempe, the author of *Berlin 1961*, it appears likely that Khrushchev believed that Soviet missiles in Cuba might pressure Kennedy into removing Allied troops from West Berlin.[55] As noted above, President Kennedy certainly made it clear at the outset that West Berlin would be protected at all costs. When Kennedy announced the discovery of the Cuban missiles, he specifically warned Khrushchev against making a *"hostile move"* against the people of West Berlin. And, as events unfolded, Khrushchev did not press the point. Although West Berlin was an island within East Germany, it remained outside of the Soviet Union's grasp.

WEST BERLIN VISIT: When JFK later went to West Berlin, he famously declared that, *"all free men, wherever they may live, are citizens of Berlin and, therefore, as a free man, I take pride in the words: Ich bin ein Berliner."* Kennedy had stood firm for the people of Berlin; and now an overflowing crowd of cheering Berliners let him know that they were grateful.

---

[55] Kempe, F., <u>Berlin 1961</u>, (N.Y.: G.P. Putnam's Sons) 2011.

President Kennedy's address to the people of Berlin
Rudolph Wilde Platz, West Berlin, June 26, 1963

AN IMPROVING EAST/WEST RELATIONSHIP: The trip to Berlin was clearly a satisfying one for JFK, but perhaps President Kennedy's most rewarding moment came when he and Nikita Khrushchev signed a Limited Test Ban Treaty in October 1963. From the first day of his Presidency, indeed, even on the campaign trail, JFK preached against nuclear testing. Soviet Russia and the United States had suspended nuclear tests between 1958 and 1961. But after their Vienna Summit in 1961, Khrushchev restarted not only underground testing but atmospheric testing as well. As you would expect, President Kennedy's advisors pushed him to do the same. Initially, JFK resisted. In a speech at the United Nations in 1961, Kennedy challenged Soviet Russia to a *"peace race"* rather than a race for nuclear weapons. Although Kennedy finally relented and reluctantly resumed nuclear testing, peace was uppermost in his mind and his heart. Our favorite JFK speech was his commencement address at American University in June of 1963, which was a call to halt the relentless and reckless nuclear arms race.

At the American University graduation ceremony, Kennedy proclaimed he wanted a peace that would <u>not</u> be: *"... enforced on the world by American weapons of war. Not the peace of the grave or the security of the slave. I am talking about genuine peace, the kind of peace that makes life on earth worth living, the kind that enables men and nations to grow and to hope and to build a better life for their children – not merely peace for Americans but peace for all men and women--not merely peace in our time but peace for all time."* He cautioned: *"War... makes no sense in an age when the deadly poisons produced by a nuclear exchange would be carried by wind and water and soil and seed to the far corners of the globe and to generations unborn."*

Commencement Address at American University
Washington, D.C., June 10, 1963

In this speech, Kennedy spoke of the Soviet Union in a way that people were not accustomed to hearing. Although deploring Communism, he urged Americans not to denigrate the Soviet people and went on to laud them for their accomplishments in many areas, including science and space. He reminded Americans that they had been our allies in World War II, suffering tremendous loss of life and property. The President said, *"And if we cannot end now our differences, at least we can help make the world safe for diversity."* He promised that this country would work *"not toward a strategy of annihilation but toward a strategy of peace."* The next day, a translation of JFK's speech was broadcast to the Soviet people and published in Soviet newspapers.

NUCLEAR TEST BAN TREATY: Since the Cuban Missile Crisis, Kennedy and Khrushchev had exchanged letters discussing how close the world had come to a nuclear catastrophe. By the time of JFK's American University speech, they had agreed to begin negotiations concerning nuclear arms. In July 1963, after less than two weeks of negotiation, an agreement was reached with the Soviets, ratified by the Senate and signed by the President on October 7, 1963.

President Kennedy signing the Limited Nuclear Test Ban Treaty
White House, Treaty Room, October 7, 1963

The Limited Nuclear Test Ban Treaty was "limited" because it excluded regulation of underground tests, which could be detected remotely. We later learned that the Soviets refused on-site international inspections because they had considerably exaggerated the number of nuclear weapons they possessed, and they didn't want this discovered.

PROMOTING CIVIL RIGHTS: The following month Kennedy

began to mend fences with his political opponents in preparation for the next year's elections. He was particularly concerned about losing the votes of Southern Democrats who were unhappy with his support for desegregation and his recent push for civil rights legislation. This was one of the reasons the President seemed so pleased with the crowds who cheered him and his wife as they took their fateful ride through Dallas, Texas on Friday, November 22, 1963.

President Kennedy had made strides in promoting civil rights. He appointed African-Americans to important federal posts and appointed Vice President Johnson to head the President's Committee on Equal Employment Opportunity. In addition, he directed the Justice Department to bring litigation against States that refused to fund desegregated schools, or in which African-Americans had been prevented from registering to vote. In 1962, the Kennedy administration sent federal troops to protect James Meredith when the University of Mississippi refused to let this black student register, even after the United States Supreme Court had ordered it to do so.

In 1963 civil rights protests again resulted in violence in Birmingham, Alabama, one of the most segregated cities in the South. George Wallace tried to prevent black students from enrolling in the University of Alabama in Tuscaloosa. This time President Kennedy not only sent federal troops to the area, he also prepared civil rights legislation that would end discrimination in public places. On June 11th, 1963, the President announced to the American people that he was sending civil rights legislation to Congress and stressed the importance of passing that legislation quickly. The President actively engaged Congress on this issue, but he met strong opposition.

John F. Kennedy addresses the nation
on Civil Rights, June 11, 1963

On November 27th, only five days after Kennedy's assassination, President Johnson addressed a joint session of Congress. He proclaimed: *"No memorial oration or eulogy could more eloquently honor President Kennedy's memory than the earliest possible passage of the civil rights bill for which he fought so long."* And yet, fierce opposition to that bill continued. After many Senate filibusters and many compromises that weakened the legislation, it was finally passed and signed into law on July 2, 1964, nearly a century after slaves had been freed from bondage.

VIET NAM: Many people wonder what President Kennedy would have done with respect to Vietnam had he been elected for a second term. Kennedy did not outline plans for further U.S. involvement in Viet Nam and the issue was still unresolved on the fateful November day in Dallas that would be his last. Two months earlier, in a September 1963 interview with Walter Cronkite of CBS, President Kennedy said that it was up to the government in South Vietnam to prosecute the war. *"We can help them, we can give them equipment, we can send our men out there as advisors, but they have to win it---the people of Viet-Nam---against the Communists."* However, in the same interview, Kennedy said that the United States should not withdraw from Viet Nam, claiming that it is an important struggle. Did he add this last point because he was up for re-election the following year and did not want to appear "soft" on Communism? We will never know.

We would like to believe that President Kennedy would have realized the war could not be won and that, if he had lived, U.S. troops would have left the area during his remaining time in office. As with civil rights, the issue of South Viet Nam was left for later Presidents to deal with. On November 22nd, 1963, the country that had been inspired by John F. Kennedy's vigor and soaring rhetoric was plunged into silence by the shock of his assassination.

The President whose museum we will visit next also lifted the mood and the spirit of the United States. Ronald Reagan's optimism and extraordinary communicative skills breathed new life into a nation that had been growing weary and despondent before his election.

Visiting JFK's Presidential Museum

Columbia Point, Boston, MA 02125

If you have a GPS device, use the following address:
220 Morrissey Boulevard, Boston, MA 02125
(note: this is not the Museum's street address.)

((617) 514-1600 or toll free: (866) 535-1960

Website: **www.jfklibrary.org**

Museum Hours:
Mon-Sun: 9am-5pm;
Closed Thanksgiving, Christmas Day and New Year's
Last introductory film of the day is at 3:55pm

Museum Admission Fees:
$14 Adults (18-61)
$12 Seniors (62+) and College Students with valid ID
$10 Ages 13-17
Free Children 12 and under

Group Visits:
Group visits of 12 people or more are eligible for a group discount
with advance reservations. Please call (617) 514-1589
Students in grades K-12 from New England Schools on an
educational group tour are eligible for free admission

Public Transportation:
Take the MBTA Rapid Transit, Red Line (any red line train) to
JFK/UMASS Station. There is a free shuttle bus to the Museum
every 20 minutes beginning at 8:00 am and running until Museum
closing. Please take the buses marked 'JFK.'

Parking
Parking is free for Museum visitors.

Accessibility

Wheelchairs are available at the Visitor Admission Desk on a first come basis. Video presentations in the Museum are captioned for hearing-impaired visitors. If you need sign language interpretation or have other needs, please call (617) 514-1569.

The Museum Café

The café serves light meals and beverages from 9:00 am to 5:00 pm daily. The café is located on the entrance level and has a maximum capacity of 45 people

Luggage Policy

Luggage, backpacks and carry-ons may not be checked at the Museum. These items can be carried with you through the Museum and might be subject to search.

Suggestions for Lodging

Boston Harbor Hotel

70 Rowes Wharf, Boston 02210
Telephone: (617) 439-7000; Website: **www.bhh.com**
Located in the financial district near Faneuil Hall and the North End where there are great Italian restaurants plus Quincy Market, Paul Revere's house, the Old North Church and more
Pets allowed; fitness center, indoor swimming pool: Free Wi-Fi; Paid parking; You might want to request a harbor view

Nine Zero Hotel, a Kimpton Hotel

90 Tremont Street, Boston, MA 02108
Telephone: (617) 772-5800; Website: **www.ninezero.com**
Pets allowed; free wi-fi; small fitness facilities;
Paid parking; Paid breakfast; Older property;
Noisy outside in the evenings; complementary wine from 5pm-6pm.

Residence Inn Downtown/Seaport

370 Congress Street, Boston, MA 02210
(617) 478-0840; Website: **www.marriott.com**
Paid parking
Free Wi-Fi (fee for upgrade to high speed), free breakfast
Pets allowed on lower floors;

Seaport Hotel

    1 Seaport Lane, Boston 02210
    (617) 385-4000; Website: www.seaportboston.com
    Located in South Boston waterfront area, adjacent to the Boston
    World Trade Center; near subway silver line to Logan airport
    Free bikes to explore the city; fitness room, indoor swimming
    pool; Pets allowed; paid parking

Encore Bed & Breakfast

    116 West Newton Street, Boston, MA 02118
    (617) 247-3425; Website: **www.encorebandb.com**
    Four rooms, all with ensuite bathrooms
    The rooms in the top floors are best re noise
    Free continental breakfast (pastries, fruit and yogurt)
    Free Wi-Fi; no parking lot; read cancellation policy on website
    No elevator and long climb to the top bedrooms on steep stairs

Suggestions for Restaurants
SEAFOOD:

Island Creek Oyster Bar:

    500 Commonwealth Ave, in Kenmore Square at the beginning of
    the campus of Boston University
    (617) 532-5300; Website: **www.islandcreekoysterbar.com**)
    Mon-Thu: 4pm-11pm; Fri-Sat: 4pm-11:30pm;
    Sun: 10:30am-11pm (morning brunch until 2:30)
    Often crowded, so best to make a reservation

B&G Oysters:

    550 Tremont Street, in Boston's south end (below street level)
    (617) 423-0550; Website: **www.bandgoysters.com**
    Hours: Mon: 11:30am-10pm; Tues-Fri: 11:30am-11pm;
    Sat: 12pm-11pm; Sun: 12pm-10pm;
    (small restaurant; usually crowded, so reservation recommended)

ITALIAN:

Coppa:

253 Shawmut Ave, in Boston's South End
(617) 391-0902; Website: **www.coppaboston.com**
Mon-Thurs: noon-10pm; Fri: noon-11pm; Sat: 5pm-11pm
Sun: 11am-10pm with brunch on Sunday from 11am-3pm;
Small restaurant: 11 indoor tables, 11 outdoor tables, 11 bar seats
Serves wood fired pizza, tapas and small plates of Italian food
Difficult to find parking on the street so only option is paid
parking

Picco:

513 Tremont, in Boston's South End
(617) 927-0066; Website: **www.piccorestaurant.com**
Mon: 11am-10pm; Tue-Sun: 11pm-11pm;
Inside and outside seating (seats 47 people);
This is a great place to take kids; no parking lot

AMERICAN:

The Parish Café:

361 Boylston Street, in Boston's Back Bay
(617) 247-4777; Website: parishcafe.com
Mon-Sat: 11:30-2am; Sun: noon-2am (can't order past 1am);
Great sandwiches; Full food menu until 1:00 in the morning
They serve alcohol; Both in and outdoor seating
Often crowded but they don't take reservations

CHINESE:

Chinatown Café:

262 Harrison Ave, China Town
(617) 695-9888
Open 7 days a week from 10:30am-8:30pm
CASH ONLY, no credit cards; no reservations

Attractions In Boston

Faneuil Hall: 1 Faneuil Hall Square, Boston, MA 02109
Part of an historic market place; Near Boston Common

Boston Symphony Orchestra:
301 Massachusetts Ave, Boston, MA
Tickets: (888) 266-1200: Website: **www.bso.org**

The Boston Children's Museum:
308 Congress Street, Boston, MA
(617) 426-6500: Website: **www.bostonchildrensMuseum.org**
Sat-Thur:10am-5pm; Fri: 10am-9pm; $14 for everyone except up to 12months old who are free (Target Friday nights: $1 5am-9pm)
Opens: noon on Xmas Day & 3pm on Xmas Eve & New Years eve;
Closed all day on Thanksgiving; call for discounted parking

Museum of Science:
1 Science Park, Boston, MA 02114
(617) 723-2500: Website: **www.mos.org**
Labor Day-Sept 1: Sat-Thu: 9am-7pm; Fri: 9am-9pm
Reg Hours: Sat-Thu: 9am-5pm; Fri: 9am-9pm; See website for pricing for admission, Exhibit Hall and Planetarium

Museum of Fine Arts:
465 Huntington Ave, Boston, MA 02115
(617) 267-9300: Website: **www.mfa.org**
Mon-Tues and Sat-Sun: 10am-4:45pm; Wed-Fri: 10am-9:45m;
Holiday closures: July 4th; Patriot's Day (third Mon in April);
Thanksgiving, Christmas Day and New Years' Day
Admission: $25 Adults; $23 Seniors (65+) and Student (18+);
$10 Youth (7-17) except Free for Youth weekdays after 3pm, weekends and on Boston public holidays; Free: kids 6 and under
 Must check umbrellas and bags & packages more than 11"x15"

Isabella Stewart Gardener Museum:
25 Evens Way, Boston, MA 02115;
(617) 566-1401: Website: **www.gardnermuseum.org**
Closed Tuesdays; open Wed & Fri-Mon: 11am-5pm; Thu: 11-9pm
Holiday closures: July 4th; Patriot's Day (third Mon in April);
Thanksgiving, Christmas Day and New Years' Day ;
$15 Adults; $12 Seniors (62+); $5 College Students; 18 & under free

RONALD REAGAN

40th President   1981-1989

First Lady: Nancy Davis Reagan

Breathtaking views of the graceful mountains and valleys of Simi Valley, California and breezes from the Pacific Ocean greet visitors walking from the parking lot to the front of the Ronald Reagan Presidential Library and Museum.

A section of the Berlin Wall stands in front of the entrance

West Berliners had decorated their side with colorful butterflies

and flowers. The opposite side is gray concrete, left that way by the dispirited East Berliners imprisoned behind it. The remnant stands here as a vivid reminder of the challenge President Reagan delivered in Berlin: *"Mr. Gorbachev – Tear down this wall!"*

From here you turn to face the California-Mission style courtyard leading into the museum.

The Ronald Reagan Museum was designed to be a "shining city on a hill," and there is a lot to see within its walls. With over 100,000 square feet of space and more than 24 galleries, it is certainly worth the trip.

EARLY LIFE: Ronald Reagan was born in Tampico, Illinois in 1911 and his family moved several times before settling in Dixon, Illinois when he was nine. His father was an alcoholic, his family was poor, and his life was stressful; however, Reagan spoke highly of his mother who had a powerful influence on him. He graduated from Eureka College in Galena, Illinois, where he majored in sociology and economics just as the country was experiencing the Great Depression. Despite getting what he admitted were poor grades in college, Reagan was able to find a job in a couple of weeks. Later he became a sports announcer and, in 1937, a Hollywood movie actor. He capitalized on a talent that later became his trademark, both as Governor of California and President of the United States: He was a "Great Communicator."

T. V. host of General Electric Theater

While in Hollywood, Reagan was elected president of the Screen

Actors Guild in 1947. He was reelected to that position every year between 1948 and 1952 and again in 1959. During those years, Reagan was active politically as a Democrat and supported a liberal woman who ran unsuccessfully for the U.S. Senate against Richard Nixon in 1950. As part of his job at the Actors Guild, Reagan tried to negotiate a deal with a union whose leaders were rumored to be Communists. That union went on strike and was so disruptive (turning over cars and buses and throwing stones) that Reagan carried a gun to work until the strike was over. Reagan was convinced that "those Communists" wanted to make trouble and therefore were not amenable to negotiating a deal with him. This was probably the start of Reagan's intense hatred toward Communism. Although we could find no proof of it, some thought that when Reagan testified to the Committee on Un-American Activity, he "named names" of those he thought were Communists in the actor's Guild. We found a transcript of his testimony and, although he did say he thought there were Communists in the Guild, he did not provide any names during that testimony.

After his acting career began to decline, Reagan got a job making speeches around the country on behalf of General Electric and hosting a TV show called, General Electric Theater. Reagan's political views became more conservative during this period. He began to listen to complaints that the Federal Government was too intrusive and that the American people were losing their freedoms, and he agreed.

FROM ACTOR TO LEADER: Reagan entered the political arena with a powerful, nationally televised speech endorsing Barry Goldwater for President during the 1964 Presidential campaign. It was an ardent call for action, pitting the populace against the "elites" in Washington, D.C. *"This is the issue of this election:"* he began, *"Whether we believe in our capacity for self-government or whether we abandon the American Revolution and confess that a little intellectual elite in a far-distant capital can plan our lives for us better than we can plan them ourselves."* Conservatives in California, who were looking for the right person to run for Governor, heard the speech and immediately tapped Reagan as the Republican candidate against the Democratic incumbent, Pat Brown.

Governor Brown dramatically underestimated his competition.

He didn't realize what a "Great Communicator" Reagan was until he saw the election results. The day after Reagan won, a reporter asked the new Governor what his agenda was going to be. Reagan joked that he didn't know because he had never played a governor before. Reagan turned out to be even more popular as Governor than he had been as an actor, working well with Democrats and Republicans. One of his major accomplishments was to reform welfare that saved California taxpayers nearly two billion dollars. However, when state spending increased, he angered conservatives by raising taxes. He also signed into law a reduction on abortion restrictions.

Almost immediately after becoming Governor, Reagan had his eye on the top job: President of the United States. He tried for the Republican nomination only 18 months after becoming Governor, but Nixon had a lock on the nomination. Reagan tried again after serving two terms as Governor by challenging the incumbent President Ford for the 1976 Republican nomination. At the Party Convention, Reagan's conservative wing of the party lost to the more moderate faction led by President Ford. Although Ford won the Republican nomination, he lost the election to the Democrat, Jimmy Carter. Ford blamed Reagan for his loss, claiming that by criticizing a fellow Republican President, Reagan turned voters away from Ford.

THE THIRD CAMPAIGN WAS A CHARM: During Jimmy Carter's term as President, Reagan continued to air his conservative views on his "Ronald Reagan Radio Commentary" series. By 1980, Reagan was ready to run for President a third time. He was determined to make Carter a one-term President and he had good reasons to assume he would be successful. Inflation was high. Interest rates had risen to double-digits. Periodic oil shortages had slowed economic growth and jobs were harder to find.

Carter lost the support of struggling farmers who turned against him for refusing to send U.S. wheat to the Soviet Union as punishment for Russia's invasion of Afghanistan. Carter also prohibited American Olympic athletes from competing in the 1980 Olympics in Russia as additional retribution toward the Soviet Union. Many Americans were also angry that Carter returned the Panama Canal to Panama, a country that was perceived to be corrupt. Topping all of those thorny issues was the most damaging of all for the Carter administration: the Iranian hostage crisis.

Grand Ayatollah Ruhollah Khomeini,

In November 1979, student supporters of the Iranian religious revolution captured 52 Americans at the U.S. Embassy in Tehran. By the time of the 1980 election, these hostages had been held for a year with little hope of being released. The Carter administration's one attempt to rescue them resulted in the loss of two aircraft and caused the deaths of eight American military men and one Iranian civilian.

THE REAGAN PRESIDENCY: Ronald Reagan's refreshing optimism invigorated voters. When he won the Presidential election in 1980, Republicans gained the majority in the U.S. Senate on his coat tails. The hostages were released from Iran on the day of Reagan's inauguration, and the nation breathed a sigh of relief.

Although the hostage crisis was over, the nation's economic crisis was still very much alive. The U.S. was suffering from "stagflation," high inflation combined with a stagnant economy, a problem that is difficult to resolve. Bringing down the rate of inflation tends to drive up unemployment, which was already at record highs. During the campaign, when Reagan advocated reducing taxes and shrinking the size of government, he frequently used the line, *"Government is not the solution to our problems; Government is the problem!"*

In his 1981 inaugural speech, President Reagan softened his rhetoric. He repeated, *"Government is not the solution,"* but this time he added: *"... it is not my intention to do away with government. It is, rather, to make it work---work for us, not over us; to stand by our side, not ride on our back. Government can and must provide opportunity, not smother it; foster productivity, not stifle it."* He was renewing a debate that had begun during George Washington's Presidency about the size and scope of the federal government. President Reagan would have sided with Thomas Jefferson against Alexander Hamilton and President Washington. Reagan was in favor of slimming down the federal government and moving more responsibility to State and local officials. However his plans were dramatically interrupted by an attempt on his life.

ASSASINATION ATTEMPT: Very early in his Presidency, Reagan had a close brush with death. On March 30, 1981 (only 70 days after Reagan's inauguration), John Hinckley, Jr., fired off six shots at the President from a handgun he had bought at a pawnshop.

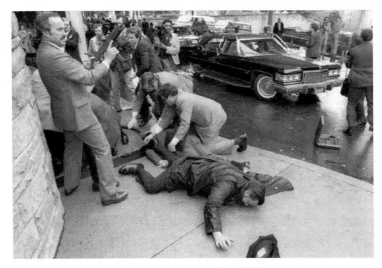

A Police Officer and Press Secretary Brady lie wounded on the ground outside the Washington Hilton Hotel, March 30, 1981

At first it was thought the President wasn't hit, however, a bullet had pierced his lung, stopping about an inch from his heart. Quick thinking on the part of the secret service and the doctors in the operating room saved Reagan's life. Before his surgery, Reagan said to the doctors that he hoped they were all Republicans. A liberal Democrat famously replied, "Today we are all Republicans, Mr.

President." This attempt on his life, rather than ending it, only increased Reagan's popularity. The President's remarkable poise and good humor drew him closer to the people.

Gun control had become an issue the prior year, after the 1980 shooting death of John Lennon. It was vigorously raised again after the attempt on Reagan's life. However, Reagan remained firmly opposed to gun related legislation during his two terms as President. It was not until after he left office that Reagan finally endorsed the Brady Bill, named after his press secretary who was paralyzed by a bullet in the head during the assassination attempt. Congress passed the Brady Bill in 1993 after (and some say because) former President Reagan had endorsed it. The Brady Bill requires a background check before a person can be issued a gun. But there are glaring exceptions. Guns can be bought and sold at gun shows and in private sales with no such precaution. There have been several attempts to get Congress to pass a more comprehensive law for background checks, but despite numerous, reputable polls showing that more than 80% of the American people favor such a law, Congress has not been willing to budge. Gun manufacturers not only give money to local and state politicians, they also prepare television and radio ads against those who don't go along with what the gun lobby dictates. Congressmen and Senators seem to care more about keeping their job than responding to the wishes of the people they serve.

HUGE TAX CUT PASSED: When President Reagan came home from the hospital to recuperate from his wounds, it was as if a hero had come back from battle. There is no doubt that a ground swell of pride in their President helped to get his huge tax cut legislation passed, even with a Democratic majority in the House of Representatives. Unfortunately, tax cuts failed to stimulate the economy as Reagan had predicted it would, and he was forced to raise taxes several times during the remainder of his Presidency.

TRAFFIC CONROLLERS' STRIKE: After showing his toughness during the assassination attempt, Reagan did so again during his first year in office when 11,000 air traffic controllers went on strike in violation of federal law. Speaking from the Rose Garden with the Attorney General at his side, Reagan stunned the nation by giving the striking workers a deadline of 48 hours to return to work or lose their jobs

President Reagan announcing ultimatum to striking Air Traffic Controllers
Rose Garden, August 3, 1981

The air traffic controllers thought they were irreplaceable and continued their strike. As the deadline passed on August 5th, President Reagan fired them all and imposed a lifetime ban on hiring anyone who joined the strike.

FIRST WOMAN APPOINTED TO SUPREME COURT: President Reagan surprised the nation again in his first year, when on July 7, 1981, satisfying a campaign pledge, he appointed Sandra Day O'Connor to be the first woman Associate Justice of the U.S. Supreme Court.

Justice Sandra Day O"Connor

SPECIAL RELATIONSHIP WITH MARGARET THATCHER:

Margaret Thatcher was the Prime Minister of Great Britain during President Reagan's two terms in office. Almost all articles about both Reagan and Thatcher point out that they had a "special relationship."

Prime Minister Margaret Thatcher

The two of them shared the same conservative goals domestically and their foreign policy went hand-in-hand as well. However, we know from our British friends that Thatcher almost lost her job when President Reagan invaded the British Commonwealth of Grenada at the end of 1983 without giving her advance warning. Can you imagine how Ronald Reagan would have reacted if Thatcher had ordered Great Britain to suddenly invade the Philippines? That is how the British viewed Reagan's action. Even the United Nations General Assembly was in an uproar. Most of its members voted for a resolution condemning the US for violating International Law. A U.S. veto prevented the UN Security Counsel from passing a similar resolution. The excuse Reagan used for the invasion was that Communists took over the government in a coup. However, the previous leaders of Grenada's government were also Communists and had also taken over the government in a coup; and Great Britain had analyzed the situation and had chosen not to interfere. In any event that was for the Prime Minister of Great Britain rather that the President of the U.S. to decide.

Reagan claimed that he was worried about Americans on the island that were going to school there. We have another theory: The Grenada invasion occurred right after many U.S. Marines were killed in a bombing in Beirut, Lebanon. Reagan had sent the Marines there as part of a UN peacekeeping force, but when their barracks were bombed, Reagan immediately abandoned their mission and brought the survivors home. With his re-election to a second term less than a year away, it may be that Reagan felt a quick and easy victory in Granada would balance his retreat in Lebanon and improve his chances in the fall election ahead. The bottom line is that aggressive acts like these make it harder for the U.S. to sanction others who do similar things. For example, although we criticize Russian President Vladimir Putin for invading Ukraine under the pretext of protecting the Russians who live there, it could be argued that the U.S. did the same thing in Granada under Reagan.

Mrs. Thatcher remained a friend to Reagan, and she may have been a role model as well. Their views on how to govern were similar. The British economy was in shambles when she became Prime Minister. Government-run industries were frequently striking, making the economy even worse. Thatcher was able to energize the British economy by privatizing some government-controlled industries and by making it illegal for the rest of them to strike unless the citizens voted for such action. She also deregulated the British financial system, which then prospered and became the envy of countries around the world. Reagan also inherited a terrible economy that he was able to turn around, and he also stood firm against a government strike and won. However when he deregulated parts of the U.S. financial system, it turned out to be a disaster.

THE SAVINGS AND LOAN CRISIS: As you can imagine, this was not a big topic at the Reagan museum. We had to do research on our own and will give only a few high lights (more like low lights) as to what happened. Prior to the 1980's, in order to encourage home ownership, "thrifts" as S&Ls were called, were permitted to pay a slightly higher interest rate on savings accounts than banks were allowed to offer, but they were only permitted to provide mortgages for home purchases. In 1980, the Carter Administration signed legislation that removed the interest rate advantage that thrifts had over banks. This hurt the S & L industry. Enter, the Reagan administration.

During Reagan's first year in office, in order to try to get thrifts on their feet again, regulations such as net worth requirements and accounting standards were dramatically eased.[56]   In addition, the Reagan administration urged regulators to *"avoid intervention and use forbearance in private markets."*[57]   In Reagan's second year, he signed a law that allowed thrifts to expand their businesses to be more like banks so that S&Ls could put their assets into commercial mortgages as well as leases and could also make loans to consumers.[58] That resulted in thrifts taking more risk with their depositors' money than the law previously allowed; and it also caused S&L's all over the U.S. to quickly change from a state chartered entity to a federal entity to take advantage of the reduced regulations and lack of oversight under the Reagan administration.

Between 1986 and the end of Reagan's Presidency in 1989, thrifts failed in droves, but this was not widely known until George H. W. Bush became President. In her book "My Father My President," Doro Bush Koch points out (through a quote from someone else) that "Reagan sort of brushed [the S&L crisis] under the rug and postponed it, but President Bush pushed for action right off the bat."[59] What Bush Sr. did was sign another one of those laws that makes it sound like our federal government is doing wonderful things for us.[60]   This law basically caused taxpayers to bail out the thrifts that still remained and to reimburse depositors for the losses, which came to between $500 billion and $1 trillion depending on who you believe. It also gave more authority to Fannie Mae and Freddie Mac (we know how that turned out). We don't know why this was not well known during the Reagan years, perhaps because the Iran Contra crisis (discussed below) was in the news or it may be that the Republicans wanted to get George Bush elected to the Presidency before the full situation was opened up to the public.

---

[56] Federal Deposit Insurance Corporation internet site; www.fdic.gov, The S&L Crisis: A Chrono-Bibliography

[57] Sherman, Matthew, A Short History of financial Deregulation in the United States (D.C.: Center for Economic and Policy Research) 2009. p.4

[58] The law was the Garn-St. Germain Depository Institutions Act of 1982 (Ibid. p.7)

[59] Bush Koch, Dora, "My Father My President (NY: Warner Books, Hachette Brook Group) 2006. p. 294

[60] The name of the law is the Financial Institutions Reform, Recovery and Enforcement Act, signed August 1989.

A SOVIET LEADER HE CAN WORK WITH: After winning his second term as President and hearing from Prime Minister Thatcher that Mikhail Gorbachev, the new General Secretary of Soviet Russia, was someone he should talk to, Reagan reached out to Gorbachev. A riveting film at the museum describes the negotiations between two men who, like Kennedy and Khrushchev before them, had the fate of the world in their hands. Reagan and Gorbachev appeared to develop a good working relationship.

ELIMINATING NUCLEAR WEAPONS: For several days in 1986, at a conference in Reykjavik, Iceland, it looked as though President Reagan and Secretary Gorbachev were going to make an historic deal to eliminate all of their respective countries' nuclear weapons. At the last minute, Gorbachev added a stipulation that the U.S. must forego pursuing the construction of Reagan's Strategic Defense Initiative or SDI (See "Peace Through Strength" below for an explanation of SDI). Reagan refused to back down. He did offer to share SDI with the Soviets, but Gorbachev rejected that compromise. Both left that meeting feeling all was lost.

After the failed Reykjavik conference, they continued to hold private discussions and, in 1987 they came together to sign an agreement that eliminated an entire class of nuclear weapons. Although not nearly as comprehensive as the treaty they had discussed at Reykjavik, Reagan was proud of this accomplishment.

Reagan greeting
Gorbachev at White House

Gorbachev and Reagan signing the
INF Treaty

Recently, the Obama White House announced that President Vladimir Putin of Russia violated this treaty by testing a cruise missile of the kind that was prohibited by the INF Treaty. In return, President Putin accused the U.S. of violating the treaty by deploying drones and testing certain other weapons, none of which were prohibited by the INF Treaty. Unfortunately, the treaty does not state what happens when the claim of a violation is made. Although international law requires that treaties must be obeyed, the reality is that there is no enforcement mechanism to punish countries that have the "clout" of Russia and the United States. It is probable that no violation of Russia will ever be adjudicated in an International tribunal. [61]

PEACE THROUGH STRENGTH: There are several exhibits in the Reagan Museum about President Reagan's new approach to the Cold War. His predecessors had aimed only to contain Communism from spreading further. As a vehement anti-Communist, Reagan did not merely want to contain Communism; he wanted to destroy it. His strategy for achieving this goal was to force the Soviet Union into bankruptcy by significantly increasing the U.S. military buildup (a 25% increase) that the Soviet Union could not match. Of course, Reagan did not just target the Soviets; he supported resistance groups fighting Communism in all parts of the world, which became known as the Reagan Doctrine.

Reagan's Strategic Defense Initiative (SDI), which was dubbed "Star Wars" by the press, was another factor in bringing an end to the Cold War. Reagan wanted to develop a sophisticated, ground-and-space-based system that would stop nuclear missiles from hitting the United States and its allies. The Soviets were nervous about having to compete with the U.S. in developing that technology. Their economy was weak and they probably had neither the expertise nor the money to build such a complex and costly system. The Soviet Union was earning less than usual from exporting its oil and also had to spend more to import food for their people due to decreasing Russian farm production. They were going broke and no one was willing to lend them money.

---

[61] Koplow, David A.,"Indisputable Violations: What Happens When the United States Unambiguously Breaches a Treaty", (The Fletcher Forum of World Affairs; Vol. 37:I) Winter 2013.

In his first term, Reagan spoke about Soviet Russia in threatening terms, referring to it as the "Evil Empire." Although many may remember George W. Bush talking about the Evil Empire, you might not have known that Reagan coined that term. In August of 1983, while Reagan was doing a sound check for his Saturday radio broadcast, he joked that he was going to "outlaw the Soviet Union forever ... we begin bombing in five minutes." Reagan didn't know that he was already live. The Soviets heard his message and some were afraid that he might mean it.[62] Cold War tensions were high. Fortunately however, the Soviets didn't act on what they had heard. In his second term, President Reagan changed his tone as he and Gorbachev developed a more cordial relationship; however, President Reagan was still firm about his unwillingness to compromise on anything: he refused to give up on SDI and he still wanted communism to be a thing of the past. As Reagan famously said about Russia, "We win; they lose". And that is exactly what happened.

THE IRAN-CONTRA AFFAIR: Unfortunately, President Reagan's legacy also includes an embarrassing scandal. The Iran-Contra Affair arose during Reagan's second term while a group with ties to Iran was holding seven Americans hostage in Lebanon. Reagan's team developed a scheme to entice Iran to release these hostages. They planned to sell weapons to Iran (to help them with their war with Iraq) in exchange for the release of the seven hostages. Lieutenant Colonel Oliver North and his boss, National Security Advisor John Poindexter planned to give some of the money earned from this weapons sale to a group called the "Contras," who were fighting the Communist Sandinista regime in Nicaragua. Remember that the Reagan Doctrine was a pledge to support any group fighting Communists around the world, so it was believed that Reagan would approve the plan to give money to the Contras. According to General Powell, who was the senior military assistant to Secretary of Defense Caspar Weinberger under President Reagan, *the President signed a top-secret 'Finding of Necessity' declaring that the covert sale of arms to Iran was in our country's interest.*[63] In other words, the President approved the first part of the

---

[62] Farris, Scott, <u>Kennedy & Reagan: Why their Legacies Endure</u> (Guilford: Lyons Press) 2013. p. 251

[63] Powell, C., Persico, J., <u>My American Journey</u>, (New York: Random House) 1995. p.311.

---

plan, the secret sale of weapons to Iran, in order to release the hostages. Powell points out that, although the President had declared that he would never deal with terrorists, this arms sale was strictly legal.

Powell also explains that neither he (Powell) nor his boss, Secretary of Defense Weinberger, nor apparently even President Reagan knew that John Poindexter and his team had sent money to the Contras in Nicaragua that had been obtained from the sale of weapons to Iran. This was definitely *not* legal. Congress had expressly forbidden it. Colin Powell acknowledges that Poindexter et al *"worked for a President who said he wanted the hostages freed and the Contras kept alive and did not concern himself with details of how it was done."*[64] The fault, he says, lies in the President's management style. Reagan was not a *"hands on"* leader as President Kennedy quickly had become after the Bay of Pigs debacle. President Reagan would let his people know how he felt about something, and then would usually let them figure out how to get the job done. Left to their own devices, the Poindexter-North team chose the wrong path. They not only engaged in illegal activity; they followed it up with a cover-up reminiscent of the Nixon era, trashing many documents and labeling others "classified" to hide the truth from Congress and the American people. Although Poindexter, North and others were charged and/or convicted of crimes in connection with Iran-Contra, none served jail time for various reasons, including a pardon provided by President George H.W. Bush, who had been Reagan's Vice President. No direct evidence has surfaced to suggest that President Reagan or Vice President Bush had any knowledge of or involvement in this scandalous affair.

THE ECONOMIC CRISIS: Although the unemployment rate climbed to over 10% in 1982, it then began to decline. According to the Bureau of labor statistics, by the end of the Reagan Presidency, unemployment had dropped to just over 5% and inflation was reduced from over 11% to 4.67%. Despite this dramatic improvement in the economy, President Reagan was disappointed that the U.S. national debt had skyrocketed during his Presidency. This was largely due to President Reagan's foreign policy of trying to bankrupt Soviet Russia by dramatically increasing the U.S. military budget. Opinion varies as

---

[64] Powell, C., Persico, J., <u>My American Journey</u>, (New York: Random House) 1995. p. 332.

to whether this tactic caused the disintegration of the Soviet Union. However there can be no denying that, in the winter of 1989, less than a year after President Reagan left office, the Berlin Wall came down. In the months that followed, the Soviet Union tottered toward collapse and the Cold War came to an end.

AIR FORCE ONE PAVILION:

The *Air Force One Pavilion* is one of the Reagan Museum's highlights. Its enormous space holds the plane that carried President and Mrs. Reagan on many of their travels during their eight years in the White House. Air Force One appears as if it's about to take off through the acre of glass that forms the window of the Pavilion. Visitors can enter the plane and walk through it from one end to the other. Visitors to this pavilion can also board Marine One, a specially outfitted helicopter used by the First Family.

POST PRESIDENCY: Several years after leaving the White House President Reagan announced that he had been diagnosed with Alzheimer's disease. On learning the news, he wrote a letter addressed to *"My Fellow Americans."* It ends with his characteristic blend of realism and optimism: *"I now begin the journey that will lead me to the sunset of my life. I know that for America there will always be a bright dawn ahead."*[65] He passed away at the age of 93 and was buried next to his Museum.

Our next and final stop will be the Presidential Museum of William Jefferson Clinton in Little Rock, Arkansas where we look at a President who perhaps didn't study the S&L disaster well enough to understand that deregulation of financial institutions has disastrous consequences for the American people. History tends to repeat itself unless we learn from past mistakes.

---

[65] Reagan, R., <u>Ron Reagan: My Father at 100</u>, (New York: Penguin Group) 2011.

Visiting Ronald Reagan's Presidential Museum

40 Presidential Drive, Simi Valley, CA 93065
(Presidential Drive is *only* accessible from *Madera Rd)*

(800) 410-8354; Website: **wwwreaganlibrary.gov**

Museum Hours:

Mon-Sun: 10am-5pm;
Closed Thanksgiving Day, Christmas Day and New Year's Day

Museum Admission Fees:

$16 Adults (18-61); $13 Seniors (62+) & College Students
$9 Youth (11-17), $6 Child (3-10);
Children age 2 and under plus active duty military are free
These prices are sometimes increased for special exhibits

Touring the Museum:

The museum is designed for self-guided touring. It is suggested by the museum that visitors allow 2 ½ to 3 hours to view all the galleries and exhibits. Tour guides (Docents) are available to tour groups of 15 or more for a fee (currently $3 per each adult, senior & child);

Groups of 20 or more:

All groups of 20 or more people <u>MUST make a reservation</u> whether or not they elect to have a tour guide; Please call (805)-577-4066 or (800) 410-8354, ext. 74066);

Parking

Parking is free; if the lot is full visitors can park on Presidential Drive approaching the museum. The museum has a limited number of bus parking spaces. All RV vehicles must park on Presidential Drive. (The parking lot is too narrow for RVs)

Accessibility

Wheelchairs are available at the Visitor Admission Desk on a first come, first served basis.

Photography:

Visitors may take pictures in the museum except inside Air Force One or at the Memorial Site. No flash pictures are allowed

DINING AT THE REAGAN MUSEUM:

Reagan's Country Café:

Can be accessed without entering the Museum:
Open Seven days a week, 9:30 am – 4:30 pm
Made to order food is available: Mon - Fri: 11am –3pm

The Reagan Pub:

Located on the first floor of the Air Force One Pavilion; Can only be accessed by visitors to the Museum. The Pub offers a selection of self-service items. Open daily 11am-4:30pm

Suggestions for Lodging

Courtyard by Marriott
191 Cochran Street, Simi Valley, CA 93065
(805) 915-5000; Website:**www.marriott.com**

Four Seasons Hotel Westlake Village
2 Dole Drive Westlake, CA 91360
(818) 575-3000; Website: **www.fours.com/westlakevillage**

Westlake Village Inn
31943 Agoura Road Westlake Village, CA 91361
(805) 496-1667;Website: **www.westlakevillageinn.com**

Hampton Inn & Suites
510 North Ventu Park Road, Thousand Oaks, CA 91320
(805) 375-0376: **www.thousandoakssuites.hamptoninn.com**

Courtyard by Marriott
1710 Newbury Road
Thousand Oaks, CA 91320
(805) 499-3900 Website: **www.thousandoakscourtyard.com**

Suggestions for Restaurants

THAI:

Thai Cottage Restaurant:
>2139 Tapo Street, Suite 117, Semi Valley, CA 93063
>(805) -306-0737 Website: **www.thaicottagesimi.com**
>Lunch: Mon-Sat: 11am-3:30pm;
>Dinner: Mon-Sat: 5pm-9pm; Sun: 3pm-9pm

KOREAN:

Korean Barbeque:
>1970 Sequoia Ave., Suite 9, Semi Valley, CA 93063
>(805) 582-1977; Open daily: 11:30am-10pm;
>Tucked away in a shopping plaza;

JAPANESE:

Sushi Tanaka:
>3977 Cochran Street, Suite D, Semi Valley, CA 93063
>(805) -306-1374 Website: **www.sushitanaka.com**
>Closed Sun-Mon; Dinner only; parking in shopping center
>Dinner: Tue-Thu: 6am-10pm; Fri-Sat: 6am-10:30pm

MEXICAN:

Taqueri Cuernavaca:
>1117 N. Ventura Ave., Ventura, CA 93001
>(805) -653-8052: Closed Tuesdays; Sun: 9am-7:30pm
>Lunch and dinner: Mon and Wed-Sat: 10am-8:30pm;

ORGANIC VEGAN:

Mary's Secret Garden:
>100 South Fir Street., Ventura, CA 93001
>(805) -641-3663 Website: **www.maryssecretgarden.com**
>Only 11 tables, so reservations are advisable
>Closed Sundays and Mondays;
>Tue-Thu: 4pm-9:30pm; Fri-Sat: 11am-9:30pm

Attractions in the Area

Simi Valley Cultural Arts Center –Live Plays by Local Actors

3050 East Los Angeles Avenue, Simi Valley, CA 93065

(805) 583-7900; Website: **www.simi-arts.org**

If you have trouble getting on the website, call the Box Office open Wednesday–Saturday: 12 Noon– 6pm (and one hour before performances for the performance that evening); The Theater is small but cozy

Playhouse & Old Town-Pasadena

39 S. El Molino Ave, Pasadena, CA 91101

(626) 356-7529; Website: **www.pasadenaplayhouse.org**

Box Office Telephone Hrs: Mon-Fri: noon-6pm; Sat-Sun: 1pm-6pm. To pick up tickets on performance day, they are open 1pm-8pm. Small theatre however you can see well from any seat and there is a lot of legroom; A few cons: the one ladies bathroom is tiny and the theater seats are old and uncomfortable (although they plan to install new seats soon). Also the theater does not have a parking lot but there is street metered parking and a paid lot nearby.

Disneyland Park –(Only 2 hours drive from Semi Valley)

1313 Disneyland Dr., Anaheim, CA 92802

(714) 781-4636; Website: **www.disneyland.com**

There are several Disney hotels. We stayed at Grand California Hotel & Spa at 1600 S. Disneyland Drive, Anaheim, CA 92802 (714) 635-2300; the hotel has a direct entrance into one of Disneyland's two Parks (California Adventure Park) There are also hotels outside the park that are cheaper, some of which have shuttle runs to Disney. The Parks open at 10am with early admission at 9am; see the website for how to get early admission

Universal Studies

100 Universal City Plaza, Universal City, CA 91600

(805) 864-8377: Website: **www.universalstudioshollywood.com**

The San Diego Zoo and Aquarium

2920 Zoo Drive, San Diego, CA 92103

(619-231-1515): Website: **www.sandiegozoo.org**

ADMISSION: Adult: $46; Child (3-11) $36; See the website about passes for multiple days or for special experiences (like getting in early to see the giant Pandas); The zoo is open every day of the year at 9am; however the closing time changes depending upon the weather and the season (earliest 5pm and latest 9pm). This year kids got in for free during the entire month of October because it is a slow time of year; you might want to check to see if they do that again next year;

Griffith Observatory

2800 East Observatory Road, Los Angeles, CA 90027

(213) 473-0800; Website: **www.griffithobservatory.org**

ADMISSION is free, but there is a charge for Planetarium shows: $7Adults ((13-59); $5 Students with ID and Seniors (60+)$3 Children (5-12): Tickets can only be purchased on site at the Observatory with Visa, Master Card or Discover Card or cash. Be aware that the museum has block scheduling: this means that tickets are given out only two or three at a time; so if you come early, don't expect to get a ticket for late in the day

OPEN 6 days a week: Tue-Fri: noon-10pm; Sat-Sun: 10am-10pm. See the website for the Planetarium shows and the times they are offered; there is a parking lot, but it tends to get filled in the evenings; overflow parking is available on the road to the parking area.

William J. Clinton

42nd President: 1993 – 2001

First Lady: Hillary Rodham Clinton

Bill Clinton may or may not be loved in Washington, D.C. or New York, but he is worshiped in Little Rock, Arkansas. The Clinton museum has lifted the city's economy. It was built on land that was the site of a run-down railroad station of the discontinued Rock Island Railroad. Although some in Congress have talked about requiring future Presidential Museums to be housed in a wing of the Smithsonian or somewhere in Washington, D.C., we are happy for Little Rock that they were able to host Bill Clinton's presidential museum. It is the engine they needed to get millions of tourists to their doorstep, increase employment and revitalize business in the downtown area.

THE CENTER & PARK: The museum is called the William J. Clinton Presidential Center and Park because it is located on approximately 28-acres of property provided by the State of Arkansas. In addition to the Museum, the old railroad station "Choctaw" was renovated and now houses the University of Arkansas Clinton School of Public Service, the Clinton Public Policy Institute and the Clinton Foundation. The Clinton museum was constructed at the edge of the Arkansas River and affords a beautiful view of the area. The old Rock

Island Railroad bridge close to the museum was renamed "Clinton Park Bridge" and has been turned into a flower-bedecked pedestrian bridge. It is fun to walk across the river on this bridge although at the present there is nothing interesting on the other side. If instead of crossing the bridge you walk along the river from the museum, you will come to the River Market District, which is now humming with customers thanks to the museum. The District is a charming strip of stores, restaurants and historic places, including at the far end, the Old State House with a collection of civil war memorabilia. Among the shops in the River Market District is the Clinton Gift Shop, the only gift shop among the Presidential Museums that we strongly recommend you visit. The inventory is unique. They sell items made by artisans in developing nations and the proceeds are returned to them.

Although we can tell you what is outside the museum, we cannot give you a first hand account of what is inside, except for the first floor and basement, which were the only places we were allowed to enter. We arrived on the first day of the 2013 federal government shutdown. The reason we were able to enter the museum at all is that, like many of the more recent museums, there are places in the museum that were not turned over to NARA (National Archives and Records Administration) and therefore are still owned by the President's Foundation. The basement is the site of Café Forty Two, a large restaurant that is open for lunch only. The first floor showcases "Cadillac One," a 1993 Cadillac limousine with protective armor that Clinton used when he was President.

We were also shown a video describing the accomplishments of the President's two terms in office. Of course, as you would expect, there was nothing in the video about his impeachment, the Whitewater affair or Monica Lewinsky. Someone watching the video asked a museum employee if those topics were covered in the exhibit halls upstairs and was told that there is an alcove where those and other unfavorable topics are discussed. Frankly, we found that, in the Museums of Presidents that are still alive, the "bad stuff" is not presented in much detail if at all. Fortunately we were paying attention to what was going on in the federal government during the Clinton administration. We have also poured through books, articles and documents about his Presidency as well as Clinton's biography, "My Life."

EARLY LIFE: William Jefferson Blythe's father was killed in an automobile accident before this future President was born on August 19, 1946 in Hope, Arkansas. Bill changed his surname when his mother married Roger Clinton. It is publicly known that Roger Clinton had a drinking problem and there were allegations of domestic violence, which may have helped to motivate President Clinton's strong support for the Violence Against Women Act, which he signed in 1994. He was well educated, attending Georgetown University, Oxford University on a Rhodes scholarship and then Yale University Law School where he met his future wife, Hillary Rodham.

PASSIONATE ABOUT POLTITICS: Hillary and Bill were married in 1975 in Fayetteville, Arkansas, where he taught at the University of Arkansas Law School. A year later he was elected as the State's Attorney General and in 1978, at the age of only 32, he was elected Governor of Arkansas. Although he lost his bid for re-election after his first term, he ran again in 1982 and that is where his reputation as the "comeback kid" began. He not only won that two-year term, but also was re-elected for three terms after that. Toward the end of 1991, he announced he was running for President of the United States. He won the Democratic nomination and ran against the incumbent President George H. W. Bush, as well as against Ross Perot who was running as a third-party candidate. Many Republicans say that Clinton won because Perot took votes away from Bush. We may never know whether that is true. Clinton won the Presidential election at the age of 46 and had responsibilities in Washington D.C. that he had never experienced as

Governor of Arkansas.

THE CLINTON LEGACY: Bill Clinton has achieved laudable goals during his post-presidency. He formed the Global Clinton Initiative (GCI), mobilizing organizations and individuals to donate large amounts of money that the GCI uses to help people around the world. In the process, he has done well by doing good, and we laud those accomplishments.

Unfortunately, we cannot give similar raves about his legacy as our President. In the remainder of this section, we will tell you why we think that his administration (with the help of Congress and at the behest of the financial institutions on Wall Street) was the prime cause for what came to be known as the Great Recession. The reason bank executives have not been going to prison for criminal behavior is that Congress and the Clinton administration saw to it that what the banks were doing was legal (with the exception of using fraudulent papers to evict people from their homes after the crisis had developed). Understanding how deregulation adversely impacted our economy will hopefully help us to enact laws that will stop that from happening again. However, we fear that adequate regulations will not be restored to protect taxpayers until we get money out of our politics.

We also believe that Clinton was responsible for the decline in U.S. manufacturing industries, and we will explain why. In case you may be thinking that we are Republican partisans, we should tell you that we are much less critical of Bill Clinton than we are of Clinton's successor. George W. Bush not only continued the Clinton policies of catering to Wall Street and benefiting those who moved manufacturing out of the U.S.; he also initiated an ill-advised invasion of Iraq that cost more than 176 *thousand* lives, 1.7 *trillion* U.S. dollars, and hurt rather than helped the United States. [66]

THE LAWS THAT ENABLED THE GREAT RECESSION:
President Clinton's administration is responsible for two laws that caused the Great Recession.[67] President Clinton not only signed these bills into law; his administration fought hard to get them passed in Congress.

THE FINANCIAL SERVICES MODERNIZATION ACT OF 1999:
This legislation is commonly known as the repeal of the 1933 Glass-Steagall Act, but we will call it "FSMA". [68] In 1998, Citicorp, one of the largest commercial banks in the U.S., merged with Travelers Group, a company that had already put together insurance companies, securities/brokerage companies and investment banks. Combining Citicorp and Travelers Group made it a "full service financial institution" which they said would modernize the financial services sector (hence the name of the act they were pushing for). The problem with their proposed conglomeration is that it violated the Glass-Steagall Act, which was still in effect. That law specified that taxpayers were

---

[66] Trotta, Daniel, "Iraq War-More than $2 Trillion" Reuters News, New York Edition March 14, 2013 (citing a study, "The Costs of War Project" by the Watson Institute for International Studies at Brown University.)

[67] We believe there would have been a recession without these two laws due to a real estate bubble because the Clinton Administration, Congress and the Federal Reserve had forced banks to offer subprime mortgages in low income neighborhoods.. However, that bubble would have only involved the U.S. and would not have been half as severe as the Great Recession..

[68] Some historians refer to the entire Banking Act of 1933 as the Glass-Steagall Act while others claim that the Glass-Steagall provisions were just the requirement of separation between commercial banks and other financial services. We therefore want to point out that the entire Banking Act of 1933 was not repealed, and that provisions such as FDIC insurance still remain.

only supposed to insure deposits placed in commercial banks, and commercial banks were required to make only conservative investments with customer deposits. By repealing Glass-Steagall and allowing commercial banks to expand their business to include insurance companies, investment banks and other similar services, the taxpayers who guarantee the FDIC insurance were suddenly (and still are) at risk of having to reimburse the loss of funds from failed, high risk investments.

Citibank and Travelers were able to merge a year before this legislation was passed because the Federal Reserve granted them a two-year waiver in order to try to get the FSMA passed so that their full service financial institution would not have to be broken apart. According to Clinton papers released recently from NARA, Citibank and Travelers were confident after hearing from some powerful politicians that Congress and the President would pass the FSMA. Being true to their word, the Clinton administration, with the help of Alan Greenspan who was the Chairman of the Federal Reserve, pushed Congress to vote in favor of this legislation. Indeed, our research shows that members of the House and Senate Banking Committees and the leaders of other congressional committees received generous campaign contributions from the financial industry during this period, leading us to conclude that Congress probably didn't need to be pushed very hard. [69] Members of Congress were not the only ones who profited from the passage of the FSMA. President Clinton's foundation received a significant amount of money from both Citibank and Bank of America, as well as money from other financial interests for the construction of his Presidential Center/museum. In addition, after the legislation was passed, Robert Rubin, Clinton's Secretary of Treasury, who lobbied hard for the FSMA, left his job at Treasury and accepted a job at Citibank in 1999 that earned him millions of dollars.

THE COMMODITY FUTURES MODERNIZATION ACT OF 2000:

---

[69] For example: Senator Gramm who was on the Senate Banking Committee had in his top 20 donors for this period Citigroup Inc., Bank of America, JPMorgan Chase & Co, Credit Suisse Group, Fannie Mae, Morgan Stanly, Dean Witter & Co, Goldman Sachs, Merrill Lynch, Capital One, Security "traders Assoc. and AIG (American International Group) netting the Senator millions of dollars. How can someone getting significant money from that group deny them what they seek to do, even if it means hurting the economy at a later time This information was obtained from the Center for Responsive Politics at OpenSecrets.org.

In a nutshell, this legislation took the derivatives that Warren Buffet famously called "weapons of mass destruction" and made them legal.[70] Derivatives had been around for a few years, but their legality was unclear. Some States had laws against them and others did not. Having been so successful with the repeal of Glass-Steagall the year before, the financial services industry again went into aggressive lobbying mode. They not only pressed for the legalization of derivatives, they also demanded that derivatives not be regulated. We vividly remember reading in the Wall Street Journal that Brooksley Born, Chairman of the Commodity Futures Trading Commission, said there would be an economic *catastrophe* if there were no regulation of over-the-counter derivatives, such as credit default swaps. She went to Congress urging them to allow her agency to regulate them. However, both Robert Rubin and Larry Summers, Rubin's successor at Treasury, argued on the side of Wall Street. Together with Alan Greenspan, they got Congress to agree that no regulation was required – even though Orange County in California had declared bankruptcy due to its risky investments in derivatives and despite that fact that a hedge fund called Long Term Capital Management (LTCM) nearly brought down the entire financial system in 1998 due to its bad bets on derivatives. Congress held hearings on LTCM and yet all but a handful of Representatives and Senators two years later voted in favor of the Commodity Futures Modernization Act. **Accordingly, when Congress and President Clinton passed that law, they substantially reduced the financial risks of their Wall Street campaign donors and transferred it to the American taxpayer.** The Act was signed at the very end of Clinton's Presidency, when George W. Bush had already been elected.

THE BLAME GAME: It took years, but our economy suffered exactly the "economic *catastrophe*" Brooksley Born had predicted. We watched in disbelief in late 2007 and early 2008, when members of Congress and Presidents Bush and Obama blamed the Great Recession primarily on the banks and secondarily on rating agencies and regulators. They took absolutely no responsibility for passing the two laws that made what the banks did legal. Or to say it another way, if those two laws had not been passed, the CEOs of the banks would now be in jail. Politicians have used their " bully pulpit" to create the myth

---

[70] A derivative is a financial contract that gets its value from the underlying asset, for example the value of a particular crop or the value of a mortgage or a packet of mortgages.

that they were as blameless as the ordinary American. We should not let them get away with that.

From 2007 until the present, President Clinton has repeatedly said he wasn't sorry for passing the FSMA (repealing Glass-Steagall), because the Federal Reserve and other regulators had already deregulated the banking industry. The law he said did not change the status quo. If that were true, there would have been no need for the Federal Reserve to give Citibank/Travelers a temporary waiver. Just recently, we heard a TV interview in which President Clinton said that repealing Glass Steagall actually helped during the Great Recession because otherwise, it would not have been legal for a commercial bank to merge with a securities firm and therefore Bear Stearns, Merrill Lynch and others would not have been saved from bankruptcy. This plainly contradicts his previous explanation that his law really did not change the status quo.

With respect to the Commodity Futures Modernization Act (CFMA), in a 2008 interview, President Clinton admitted that he had made a mistake in signing that act. The next day Clinton representatives backtracked on that admission. A couple of months later, we watched a conference on C-span in which Clinton said his team had researched whether an act during his term in office was responsible for the Great Recession and found that the answer was "no". What was strange is that the moderator didn't follow up on Clinton's statement, not even to ask what act or acts he had researched. It was as though he had been told in advance not to pursue this subject. From then until 2010, Clinton maintained that his administration had no responsibility for the Great Recession.[71] However in 2010, when major newspapers and magazines started reporting that the FSMA and CFMA had been responsible for the Great Recession, Clinton confessed he was wrong to have signed the 2000 law, and blamed it on the advice of Bob Ruben and Larry Summers as well as the Bush administration for *"scaling back on policing the financial industry."*[72] However, Clinton

---

[71] In 2009, Ann Curry told Clinton that she had been reading that he had some responsibility for the recession. He replied with a question: "...did any of them [the writers of the articles] seriously believe that if I had been President and my economic team had been in place for the last eight years that this [the recession] would be happening today? And I think they know the answer; that's wrong. No". See Amy Goodman & Juan Gonzalez, "A Daily Independent Global News Hour" (democracynow.org,: February 17, 2009).

also said that if he had not signed the CFMA, the majority of Republicans in Congress would have passed it over his veto, as if to say that his signature did not matter! [73] What we found interesting is that neither of these major laws that Clinton fought hard to pass was mentioned in his book, "My Life."

LIFTING THE UNITED STATES ECONOMY: It is not a myth that the Clinton Administration lifted the economy. Clinton credits cutting federal spending and raising taxes as the causes of this improvement. As to the latter, he claims he only raised taxes on the rich, but it was Clinton who began the tax on Social Security. In fact, during President Clinton's administration, Social Security paid less to recipients in benefits than it received from taxes; and Social Security taxes are certainly not just paid by the rich. Clinton did something else with Social Security that is not widely known. He used money held in the Social Security trust fund to pay for government expenditures. In effect, he balanced the budget by increasing our government's debt to the Social Security trust fund. When President Clinton claims that the government had "surpluses" under his watch, people tend to believe that he lowered the national debt. In fact, from January 30, 1993 (just after his inauguration) until the end of his Presidency, the national debt rose by 1.6 Trillion dollars, from 4.16 trillion dollars ($4,167,200,410,899.83) to 5.7 trillion dollars ($5,740,291,126,546.45).[74] That is not too bad when compared to what happened under the next two Presidents, but President Clinton cannot claim to have lowered U.S. debt. When President Clinton states in his book "My Life", that he created a surplus, it seems disingenuous not to acknowledge that, in order to create a *budget* surplus, he borrowed money from the Social Security trust fund and added to the *national* debt.

---

[72] Harris, Evan, "Clinton: I was wrong to listen to wrong advice against regulating derivatives" (ABCnews.go.com: April 17, 2010).

[73] Harris, Evan, "Clinton: I was wrong to listen to wrong advice against regulating derivatives" (ABCnews.go.com: April 17, 2010).

[74] You can see the amount of the national debt at **www.treasurydirect.gov**. In the search box at the top right type: "public debt in 1993", and a new screen will appear. Click on "Debt to the Penny (Daily History Search Application). When you enter your dates the national debt for that period will be shown.

THE DECLINE OF U.S. MANUFACTURING: During the 1992 Presidential campaign, Mr. Clinton declared that he would not go forward with NAFTA (North American Free Trade Agreement) that had been negotiated by his predecessor, George H. W. Bush with Canada and Mexico. However, after he was elected, Clinton not only cemented those deals, he also signed trade deals with many other countries, telling the American people that trade deals bring jobs to the U.S.   However, those trade deals were better for foreign trading partners than for the United States.   As a result of those trading agreements, jobs were lost rather than gained in all 50 states and the District of Columbia."[75]. U.S. imports rose and exports fell, producing huge U.S. trade deficits. According to the Trade and Globalization Report, the trade deficit with Mexico and Canada rose from $30 billion in 1993 to $85 billion in 2002 (all figures in inflation-adjusted 2002 dollars), an increase of 281%. The Center for Economic and Policy Research (CEPR) wrote that the overall 2000 trade deficit set a new record high, with an annual rate of $399 billion, equal to 4% of GDP. They wrote that the trade deficits in the last four years of the Clinton presidency led to huge job losses in the well-paying manufacturing industries.[76]

However, the most severe hit to the economy was the granting of Permanent Normal Trade Relations (PNTR) to China at the end of Clinton's presidency in 2000. A detailed report distributed in 2012, "The Surprising Swift Decline in U.S. Manufacturing Employment," found that by giving China PNTR, not only did many manufacturers move their business overseas, but many stopped manufacturing domestically. According to this report, rather than the predicted 10% rise, this caused a decline in manufacturing between 2001 and 2007of more than 15%.[77] Both President Clinton and Alan Greenspan fought hard to get PNTR passed by Congress because *"this will doubtless*

---

[75] Scott, Robert E., "The High Price of 'Free'Trade: NAFTA'S Failure has cost the United States jobs across the nation," **www.epl.org** November 17, 2003.

[76] Baker, Dean, "2000 Trade Deficit Sets New Record" Center for Economic and Policy Research: February 21, 2001.

[77] Pierce, Justin R. (Board of Governors of the Federal Reserve) and Schott, Peter K. (Yale School of Management) National Bureau of Economic Research, 2012 Report.

promote internal economic development…and contribute to lifting its [China's] citizens out of poverty…plus will work to strengthen the rule of law in China." The President and the Chairman of the Federal Reserve forgot which country they were supposed to protect.[78] The only reason America has been able to sustain the high trade deficit that resulted from the trade deals is because the United States holds the world's reserve currency: Foreigners buy US bonds, allowing Americans to buy foreign products.[79] However, if Ted Cruz and his Tea Party comrades again refuse to lift the debt ceiling, countries may choose a different reserve currency, driving this country into a recession or worse. Some countries, including China, have already started to do so. The bottom line is that during Bill Clinton's first term, the economy improved and many service jobs were added; however, by the end of his Presidency, he had put the U.S. on a path that would hurt the economy much more than help it, even if the Great Recession had not occurred.

---

78 **www.cbsnews.com** "Clinton, Greenspan: China Belongs," May 18, 2000)

[79] Smil, Vaclav,"The Manufacturing of Decline" The Breakthrough Institute **www.thebreakthrough.org**. May 23, 2012).

William J. Clinton
Presidential Center & Park

1200 President Clinton Ave., Little Rock, AR 72201

(501) 374-4242   Website: www.clintonlibrary.gov

Museum Hours:
> Mon-Sat: 9am-5pm; Sunday: 1pm-5pm
> Closed Thanksgiving Day, Christmas Day and New Year's Day
> Café 42: Lunch: Mon-Fri: 11am-2pm; Coffee: Mon-Fri: 9am-4pm

Museum Admission Fees:
> $7 Adults (18-61) : $3 Children (6-17), under 6 are free
> $5 Seniors (62+), College Student & Retired Military (need IDs)
> July 4th and August 19 (Clinton's Birthday) are free days for all
> UACS Faculty & staff and all active duty military are free

Group Visits:
> School groups with reservations are free; Adult groups of 20 or
> more get reduced rate of $5 per adult with reservations.
> For reservations contact Volunteer and Visitor Services Office at
> (501) 748-0419

Tours:
> Hand-held audio tour is available to rent for $3; guided tours
> must be reserved a least 14 days in advance (501) 748-0419.'

Parking
> Parking is free for Museum visitors..

Accessibility
> Wheelchairs are available at the Visitor Admission Desk on a first
> come, first served basis.

Suggestions for Lodging

Capital Hotel
> 111 West Markham Street, Little Rock, AK 72201
> (501) 374-7474; Website: **www.capitalhotel.com**
> Located downtown in the River Market Area,
> Near the Clinton Presidential Center & Park
> Free Wi-Fi; bar/lounge;
> Great restaurant (Ashley's, see below);
> Paid parking; no pets

Residence Inn Little Rock
> 219 River Market Ave., Little Rock, AK 72201
> (501) 376-7200; Website: Marriott.com/LITRD
> Near the Clinton Presidential Center & Park
> Paid parking; Pets welcome ($100 fee);
> Free Wi-Fi; free breakfast; light dinner Mon-Wed: 6-7:30

Robinwood Bed & Breakfast
> 2021 South Arch Street, Little Rock, AK 72206
> (501) 372-0999; Website: **www.robinwoodbnb.com**
> Parking on street: 5 rooms with ensuite bathrooms
> Free Wi-Fi; free breakfast

The Empress of Little Rock
> 2120 Louisiana Street, Little Rock, AK 72206
> (501) 374-7966; Website: **www.theempress.com**
> Victorian House with ensuite bathrooms;
> Also available carriage house with modern ensuite bathrooms
> Free breakfast; free Wii-Fi; free parking area

Suggestions for Restaurants

Ashley's at the Capital Hotel:

111 West Markham Street, Little Rock, AK 72201

(501) 370-7011; Website: **www.capitalhotel.com** and click on "dining"

Located downtown in the River Market;

Breakfast: Mon-Fri: 6:30am-10am; Sat-Sun: 6:30am-11am

Lunch: Mon-Fri: 11:30am-2pm; Brunch on Sun: 10am-2pm

Dinner: Mon-Thurs: 5:30am-9pm; Fri-Sat: 5:30am-10pm

Paid valet parking

EUROPEAN: (GERMAN & CZECH)

The Pantry:

11401 Rodney Parham Road, Little Rock, AK 72212

(501) 353-1875; Website: **www.littlerockpantry.com**

Lunch: Mon-Fri: 11am-4pm;

Dinner: Mon-Sat: 4pm-Midnight; reservations only for at six people and over; Smoking on the patio after 10pm

CHINESE: (TAIWANESE)

Mr. Chen's Authentic Chinese Cooking:

3901 S. University Ave., Little Rock, AK 72204

(501) -562-7900; Website: **www.mrchenschinese.com**

Sun-Thu: 11am-9pm; Fri-Sat: 11am-9:30pm;

Free parking lot

It's inside a grocery store so if your looking for ambience, this is not the place for you; take-out is available

BARBEQUE

Whole Hog Cafe:

2516 Cantrell Road, Little Rock, AK 72202

(501) 664-5025; Website: www.**wholehogcafe.com**

Lunch & Dinner: Mon-Sat: 11am-8pm

Free parking

Attractions in Little Rock

Farmers Market:
  400 President Clinton Ave, Little Rock AK 72201
  Saturdays: 7am-3pm, rain or shine
  May through October (Exact dates can be different each year)
  Located in downtown area in two outside pavilions

Little Rock Central High School National Historic Site:
  2120 W. Daisy L. Gatson Bates Drive, Little Rock AK 72202
  (501) 374-1957: call this number to sign up for a free guided tour;
  You should do that as much in advance as you can because there
  are only two trips a day
  The National Park Services Center opens daily: 9am-4:30pm
  Closed Thanksgiving Day, Christmas Day and New Years Day
  Tells the story of desegregation in 1950's, especially about the
  Little Rock 9 who finally were admitted to the school in 1957
  The high school is still active so please only go into the Visitor's
  center; there you will find exhibits and Rangers who will answer
  your questions. Website: **www.nps.gov/chsc**

Esse Purse Museum:
  1510 Main Street, Little Rock, AK 72202
  (501) 916-9022
  Website: **www.essepursemuseum.com**
  Tues-Sun: 11am-4pm; Closed Mondays
  Free Parking lot

MacArthur Museum of Arkansas Military History:
  503 East Ninth Street, Little Rock AK 72202
  (501) 376-4602
  Mon-Sat: 9am-4pm; Sun: 1pm-4pm
  Located downtown in MacArthur Park
  A lot of history about MacArthur and several wars in a small area
  Also see the Arkansas Korean War Veterans Memorial there
  Free parking and free admission

Arkansas Arts Center:

> 501 E. 9th Street, Little Rock, AK 72202
> (501) 372-4000
> Website: **www.arkansasartscenter.org**
> Tues- Sat: 10am-5pm; Sun: 11am-5pm; Closed Mon & holidays
> Located downtown in MacArthur Park
> Free parking and free admission

Little Rock Zoo

> 1 Zoo Drive, Little Rock AK 72205
> (501) 666-2406
> Website: **www.littlerockzoo.com**
> Daily from 9am-5pm (last admission is 4pm);
> Closed Thanksgiving, Christmas Day and New Years Day
> Admission: $12 Adults: (13 to 59); $10 Seniors (60+);
> $9 Children (1-12); Free for children under 12 months
> Parking: Currently $2 per vehicle

NOTES:

Suggestions from the Authors:

Before visiting a museum, restaurant or other facility listed in this book, please contact it directly using the information provided in the Travel Tips section to ascertain whether the hours of operation, prices or other information published here has changed. Also, inquire about upcoming special events you might want to see. Make sure that no private parties have been scheduled that could cause early closings or otherwise limit public access. We have noticed that Presidential Museums have begun to rent out their property to private parties in the evening, causing the museum to occasionally close earlier than normal.

We have included more bed and breakfast lodgings in this Second Edition than in the First Edition because we found their pricing is generally cheaper than hotels. B&Bs are also usually more fun in terms of meeting people on your trip. However, there are pros and cons to both types of lodging. For example:

Breakfast: Virtually all B&Bs include breakfast in their pricing, but some serve only a continental breakfast such as pastries while others have hot meals such as eggs, omelets, pancakes and French toast. Many hotels now provide free breakfasts as well, but we often find that the hotel breakfasts are of lesser quality than the home-cooked meals served by the B&Bs and they lack the charming atmosphere and personal attention typical of Bed and Breakfast Inns

Smoking/Pets/Children: We did not specify "no smoking" in this edition, since smoking is now prohibited in almost all restaurants, bed and breakfasts and hotels. We mention smoking only when it is allowed, for example on outdoor patios of some restaurants and special rooms or floors of some hotels. All of the B&Bs we have stayed in did not allow smoking or pets, and many don't allow young children below a particular age, with some not permitting any children at all.

Ensuite bathrooms: Many B&Bs do not have ensuite bathrooms for all of their guest rooms. Please make sure you ask about that because it is not always clear from their website. A guest in a B&B we stayed in was angry because his bathroom, although private, was down the hall. If it would be an unpleasant surprise for you to learn that you need to share a bathroom with strangers, be sure to ask that question before booking.

Cancellation Policy and mandatory pre payments: We believe this is the most troubling part of booking with a B&B. Their cancellation policies are extremely variable and generally much less flexible than those of hotels. We once booked with a B&B that charged a penalty for cancelling a couple of months in advance. We have also found that most B&Bs charge a small fee up front that is nonrefundable even if you cancel before a penalty would kick in. **Reading the cancellation policy on the B&B's website is a must**. If they don't have a website, we suggest that you have them send you their cancellation policy **in writing** by fax or email. A couple of times we have had a B&B change the cancellation policy that they had previously given us orally.

Miscellaneous: We always inquire about whether a B&B has Wi-Fi. We find that many don't, but if they do, a B&B owner has never asked us to pay for it. We have found that all hotels we have stayed in during the past several years have Wi-Fi, and some require additional payment for that. We have never seen a B&B with an elevator, so those who don't do well walking up steps should be warned. B&B bedrooms often will be smaller than the hotel rooms we stay in, but that is definitely not always the case.   Many B&B's have king size beds with good-sized rooms.

A word about Presidential Museums:

Franklin Roosevelt was a great lover of history and was the first to build his own Presidential Museum and Library. He not only wanted to preserve his papers for prosperity but also to showcase his many collectors' items as well as gifts he had received while in office.

Before FDR, Presidents took their papers home with them, often storing them in attics or basements. Although some of these records were preserved, many were lost to history. Using private funds, FDR built a library on his family's property in Hyde Park, New York to provide a place where historians could find a complete record of his Presidency. He donated the completed building and all of his presidential papers and materials to the National Archives and Records Administration (NARA} to be maintained and operated with taxpayer funds. When Harry Truman wanted to do the same thing, Congress passed a law allowing the two living presidents, Truman and Hoover, and all future presidents to donate their papers to the federal government rather than to their relatives or other private parties who might lose them or place them where they would not be seen by the public. In 1979, when it was learned that President Nixon was trying to destroy his White House papers and tape recordings, it became mandatory for presidents to donate their papers to NARA.

PRIVATE MUSEUMS: Before FDR opened his Museum and Library, many local communities had created museums for former presidents who had lived in their area, often by transforming his family home into a public exhibit. These served the dual purposes of preserving history and attracting tourists. One of these was George Washington's Mount Vernon, an estate that was neglected and falling into disrepair when it was purchased in 1858 by a group of women called the Mount Vernon Ladies' Association of the Union. Accepting private donations from around the country, this determined organization restored the grounds and home and continues to maintain and operate this historical treasure as a haven for tourists as well as academicians. Similarly, the Lincoln Presidential Museum and Library in Springfield is operated by the Illinois Historic Preservation Agency; and the Woodrow Wilson Presidential Library Foundation operates the Wilson Presidential Museum in Staunton, Virginia.

FEDERALLY OPERATED MUSEUMS: Following FDR's example, subsequent presidents began accepting donations to build their own library/museum while still in office. After the building is completed, it is handed over to NARA to maintain and operate with taxpayer funds. All of the museums discussed in this book, except for the three private museums mentioned above, are part of the Presidential Libraries System administered by NARA.

The funds solicited from donors to build the structures are held in private foundations, and the donations are not disclosed to the public. The secrecy of the donors' identity became a matter of concern when President Clinton gave a pardon to Marc Rich who had been indicted on tax evasion. It subsequently became known that Mr. Rich's ex-wife had donated generously to President Clinton's museum. Although there is no evidence that the donation was a quid-pro-quo for the pardon, it made people wonder about the funding of these museums. Several legislative bills have been proposed that would require presidents to disclose the names of the donors to their museums and the amounts of their donations. However, until now these measures have failed.

There has also been discussion about centralizing Presidential papers and memorabilia within the Smithsonian Museums in order to reduce the amount that taxpayers must spend to operate and maintain separate museums, a cost that is nearing $80 million a year. Recent museums have each become grander than its predecessors. In 1986 Congress required that the private foundation for each president's museum contribute to the cost of its continuing maintenance and operation. George W. Bush's foundation had to contribute 20% of the cost of building his museum for future upkeep; Barrack Obama's foundation will need to provide 60% of the cost of his building for this purpose.

At the end of our journey we found that the touch of skepticism we felt at the outset was unfounded. Presidential Libraries and Museums not only preserve critical lessons of history; they also vitalize the economies of communities around the country that host and serve the travelers who come to see them. We encourage you to enjoy a memorable visit to one or more of these national treasures.

Please send your comments or questions to:
presidentialguidebook@yahoo.com.